STOLEN LAND

DEDICATED TO THE ALLEGANY STATE PARK HISTORICAL SOCIETY

STOLEN LAND

LARRY BEAHAN

COYOTE PUBLISHING OF WESTERN NEW YORK
5 DARWIN DRIVE
SNYDER NEW YORK 14226
LARRY_BEAHAN@ROADRUNNER.COM

2018

ACKNOWLEDGEMENTS

The material compiled in this book is based largely on my rough notes taken at meetings of the Allegany State Park Historical Society. The quotations from those meetings are approximate.

The societies hard work, the excellence of their speakers and the good graces of the Park and its staff provided this incomparable opportunity.

Larry Beahan

CONTENTS

INTRODUCTION

Is Allegany State Park stolen land? Ask the people who owned farms and homes in the vicinity when New York State decided to expand the Park.

Do the waters of the Kinzua Reservoir conceal stolen Seneca land? Ask the Senecas.

Was North America stolen from the Indians who made their homes here before Europeans arrived? Ask Chief Red Jacket, whose portrait graces the cover of this book. He and many, many others living and dead would answer, "yes" to all three of these queries.

This book, "Stolen Land," takes its title from its first chapter. The chapter was based on a talk given to the Allegany State Park Historical Society by anthropologist and Salamanca native Doctor Sidney Horton. He reviewed the Federal government's Dawes Act, its Burke Act and the violations of Indian treaty after Indian treaty. Just between 1871 and 1934, these laws and illegal acts resulted in Native American tribes losing, to white settlers, over 90 million acres, an area the size of Montana.

Tyler Heron tells a firsthand story of the Seneca Nation's losing struggle to the Federal Government in the 1960s. The United States confiscated a third of the Seneca Reservation for the construction of Kinzua Dam and Reservoir.

Sidney Horton's and Tyler Heron's talks led me to research my own ancestral family's involvement in this struggle for land ownership. The chapter, titled "Minnetinka," is named for an Indian orphan of the 1675 King Philip's War. This war was an attempt by united New England tribes to drive the English colonists out of the Indian homeland. She is the link between the Native American and the European branches of my own family.

The speakers at Allegany State Park Historical Society meetings brought their intimate knowledge of the Park and of the surrounding Seneca Nation, the peoples of those lands and the lands themselves. Taken as a whole the voices heard in this book, "Stolen Land," tell a considerable portion of the troubled history, the possession and the dispossession of this microcosm of the North American Continent, Allegany State Park.

Tom Cain and Theresa Attea represent white families that were successors to loggers who in turn had succeeded Indians in ownership of land that became Allegany State Park. Tom and Theresa described idyllic lives on a farm and in a summer home before their lands were taken from them for Park expansion.

In contrast, David Carr and his brothers and sisters grew up in equally idyllic circumstances in one of the snug homes provided by the Park for Park workers.

Janice Gordon France came from a Seneca family and married into the Frances, an old white Allegany family. Some of the France family still lives on an inholding at the center of the Park and they cherish it.

Over time, there has been a melding of races and uses of the Park. The Hawk Creek animal rescue experts display eagles, owls, porcupines and a skunk in the Park, their natural habitat. Corey Dowdy demonstrates the Snow Snake game, still vigorously contested by Senecas in and around the Park. The Art Roscoe Cross-country Ski Area is thronged in winter with followers of that European sport.

Park Commissioner, Hugh Dunn, takes us to undiscovered corners of the Park and Larry Kilmer reveals its surprising railroad archeology. Sally Marsh spins stories of Hootenannies that have supplanted Seneca Dances… at least inside the Park.

The story of the restoration of the Wild Turkey to Allegany hints at a return to the original state of this land.

Then, in Chapter 15, the beautiful cedars that greeted us on Red House Dam, as we approached the iconic Administration Building, are cut down…with no explanation.

In 2010, after decades of conflict and debate between advocates for timber, oil, recreation and preservation, the users of the Park arrived at a grand compromise, the long-awaited Master Plan.

In "Stolen Land's" last Chapter, "250 Miles of Trail," the Park applies this compromise to its massive trail system. It guarantees the preservation of the forest and prescribes how much of the forest can be used to accommodate man. It does not return the land to former owners.

STOLEN LAND

Seneca Chief Red Jacket

On a brilliant, unusually warm February day a few fisherman challenged the ice on Red House Lake as Doctor Sidney Horton spoke to the Allegany Historical Society meeting at Camp Allegany. The talk had been advertised as a discussion of Charles E. Congdon's book, "Allegany oxbow; a history of Allegany State

Sidney Horton PhD.

Park and the Allegany Reserve of the Seneca Nation." Horton focused on his area of expertise as an ethnologist: How we Europeans have dealt with our stealing of Seneca lands.

Horton offered the rare perspective of a Suny Buffalo-trained PhD anthropologist who grew up in Salamanca, in the middle of the Seneca Allegany Reservation on the edge of Allegany State Park during the heat of battle between the Seneca Nation and the United States Federal Government over three expropriations of Seneca land. He has the added perspectives of being the descendant of an industrialist family that had exploited these lands and of having many Seneca friends including former Seneca Nation President George Heron.

As old Allegany hand, Bill Weitzel, began introducing Doctor Horton, Bob Byledbal, a former Park Concessionaire shouted a request, "Ok to call you Sid?" Our speaker nodded and waved affably to his old friend, possibly a former employer of his. Many Salamanca kids worked in Bob's dancehalls and stores.

Bill Weitzel's introduction went like this, "Sid is a good neighbor of mine. He has the property just north of me on the old Park-entrance road. I've known him all his life. I coached him in midget football. He was the most popular member of the team… not because he was such a good player but because he had such good looking sisters."

Horton, mid-sized, middle-aged, wearing a suit coat and a collarless shirt chuckled, "I've known Bill since I was a little kid. He was old even then. It was great growing up in Salamanca. It was like growing up in Mayberry. Bill once approached me to run for elective office. I turned him down. I told him, 'You know those skeletons you've got in your closet? Well, I've got graveyards in mine.'

"A lot of my friends were Allegany ski jumpers."

Here he showed slides of ski jumpers including a comic shot of one of his friends supposedly at the brink of a takeoff with mouth and eyes wide in fright or astonishment.

After another laugh, he began with a serious tone, "My training is as an Ethno-Historian, that's a subdivision of Anthropology. We study anything humans do or have done. As part of the job, I once read every issue of the 1939 Salamanca Republican."

In an aside he added, "It's also a cheap way to travel.

"My family were industrialists. My great grandfather owned a tannery in Salamanca. We had tanneries all across Western New York. We denuded these hills for the tannin in the bark of their hemlocks. The logs were floated down the Allegany and Ohio Rivers to be sold in Pittsburgh, or even New Orleans."

Log Raft

He flashed a picture on the screen of a huge log raft with a small house built on it, floating in the River.

"Senecas from the Cornplanter Reserve were the experts in running these rafts. Some of the rafts covered several acres.

"When I was young, I spent a lot of time in the Park. Charles Congdon was a Park Commissioner and a friend of my father's. He showed me around, showed me where Sweetwater is. Besides "Allegany Oxbow," he helped write a three-volume history of Western New York.

"This year the 70th Iroquois Research Conference was held in Rochester, New York. The first of these Iroquois Ethno-History conferences met in the Red House Administration Building in 1945. It was organized by Charles Congdon, William Fenton and Merle H. Deardorff. The father of Ethno-History is Lewis H. Morgan. He began the work with the Senecas."

General John Sullivan

Horton's brief mention of Morgan led me to the following information gleaned from the internet:

Lewis H. Morgan (1818-1881) was an anthropologist as well as a New York State Assemblyman from Rochester. He lived for a time among the Senecas, the Keepers of the Iroquois Confederation's Western Door. He learned their language and was adopted into the Hawk clan. He is noted for his Ethnography of the

Iroquois and his theory that the matrilineal clan, as practiced among the Senecas, was the earliest form of human societal organization. His ideas influenced Marx, Darwin and Freud.

William N. Fenton (1908 – 2005) followed in Morgan's footsteps as the leading scholar of his time studying Iroquois history and culture. Fenton, too, lived with the Senecas and was adopted into the same clan as Morgan. He was director of the New York State Museum and a professor of anthropology at the State University of New York where he guided many students of the Iroquois. Karl Marx and Friedrich Engels, his contemporaries, were influenced by reading his work on social structure, material culture and the influence of technology on progress.

Horton showed us a slide of John Mohawk, a recent SUNY Buffalo Professor of Anthropology and a student of Iroquois culture. He continued, "One of the first things taught in ethnography is to avoid ethno-bias. Continuously, for thousands of years, until about 1800 transportation was by horse, heat was from burning wood and we earned our living tilling the soil. Suddenly we entered the machine age. Our culture made the machine the measure of progress along with the ability to speak English, the practice of Christianity and the concept of land ownership. With this ethno-bias, we Europeans saw Senecas and other Native Americans as backward. Our superior culture seemed to justify taking their land.

"Government policy became, move the Indians west of the Mississippi where they can fight and kill each other. The Indian Removal Act of 1830, signed by President Andrew Jackson, made that policy law.

"But even that didn't satisfy European land hunger. Indian lands had been owned in common by all members of the tribe. The Dawes Act of 1887 empowered the President of the United States to divide up reservations and assign land allotments to individuals. While this was supposed to bring Indians up to the standard of European culture in land ownership, it resulted in unscrupulous whites buying much of the reservation land.

"The Dawes Act exempted the five "Civilized Indian Nations: Cherokee, Chickasaw, Choctaw, Creek and Seminole.

Seneca lands also escaped, because the Holland Land Company had purchased the right to own them.

CHEROKEE

CHOCTAW

MUSCOGEE
(CREEK)

CHICKASAW

SEMINOLE

Five Civilized Indian Nations

"Justification of the Dawes Act was reinforced by the Gallagher Report of 1889. Its survey of Indian reservations called the culture morally corrupt, Indians thin and impoverished, their women immoral, their men not caring and the reservations full of fighting and crime. A subsequent report by Whipple found the Gallagher Report almost totally erroneous.

"A commission during Teddy Roosevelt's Presidency denounced 'the existence, within our territory, of foreign nations whose practices are repugnant.' Yet thousands thronged the Pan American Exhibition to glimpse Senecas living in a longhouse, celebrating their culture. So Seneca culture is repugnant but it's ok for our entertainment? The federal government was on a mission to stamp out Indian culture and force Indians to assimilate European culture."

I went back to the internet and gathered a list of additional federal actions taken toward breaking the power of the tribes: The Dawes Commission set up in 1893, attempted to force the previously exempt, Five Civilized Tribes to accept the land allotment system. The Burke Act of 1906 forced U.S. Citizenship on tribes that didn't want it. The Curtiss Act of 1908 ended tribal jurisdiction over Indian land.

From 1871 to 1934, Native American tribes lost over 90 million acres to white settlers. Senecas lost the Buffalo Creek Reservation and lands along the Genesee. Some dispossessed Senecas relocated in the west. But many remained on the Cattaraugus, Tonawanda and Allegany Reserves.

Horton said, "The fight to get the half-mile-wide strip along the Allegany River away from the Senecas was endless."

He showed a slide of the Allegany reservation.

Then he went on, "Senecas have a great sense of place. The 1890 census of the Allegany reservation contains most of the same names that are there now. Names like Tallchief. The population has remained stable at about 1000 from the beginning of the 1800's till now. Women are named in the census as the heads of households since Senecas are a matrilineal society.

"At one time the Senecas raised a protest for being charged a ten dollar and fifty cent "Alien" hunting fee rather than the one dollar charged US Citizens. They did not believe they were Aliens and they did not wish to be Citizens of the United States. A letter to the editor of the Salamanca paper In 1902 by an Indian named Leroy Pierce protested the Dawes land allotment system and U.S. citizenship for Indians. He demanded a Seneca voice in Seneca affairs."

     Again to get a fuller understanding of these complex issues that Doctor Horton tried to pack into the brief time we allotted him, I took a look into Seneca history. During the American Revolution the Iroquois tribes split their allegiance. Tuscaroras and Oneidas sided with the Americans, the Seneca and the rest of the Confederation joined the British.

     Early in the war General George Washington told American settlers along the Mohawk Valley and in Western New York to form militias for their own defense. British and Indian raiding parties took a heavy toll on them. In the summer of 1779 Washington sent Major General John Sullivan and Brigadier peace offerings until the Seneca villages and means of sustenance were destroyed. General James Clinton with a large force to punish the Senecas and their allies. Washington ordered his generals to accept no

Castle at Fort Niagara
Photo Courtesy of Ad Meskens

The Senecas retreated to the inadequate shelter of the British at Fort Niagara where many died of starvation and exposure. It was a stunning defeat.

After the war, at Fort Stanwix in1784, the United States forced a treaty on the Iroquois which established the boundary for the first American Indian reservation in the United States. The treaty recognized each of the six nations as sovereign nations, and promised to protect the reserve's land.

In 1788 Oliver Phelps and Nathaniel Gorham purchased, from Massachusetts, preemptive rights to most of what later became Western New York. They ran out of money before they had completed their payments or extinguished the Iroquois rights to the land. Robert Morris, a signer of the Declaration of Independence and the, then, richest man in the United States, bought the Phelps Gorham lands in 1791 and shortly sold the western two thirds of it to a Dutch syndicate, the Holland Land Company.

Before the Dutch deal could be completed, Iroquois rights had to be dealt with. To that end the 1797 Treaty of Big Tree was negotiated near present day Geneseo. Morris, the Holland Land Company, a US Commissioner and 3000 Iroquois including Red Jacket and Cornplanter met there. The Indians sold 3.75 million western New York acres, retained 200,000 acres and were paid $100,000 (about $1.39 million today).

In the Buffalo Creek Treaty of 1842 the Senecas sold that reservation and the Tonawanda Reservation to Thomas L. Ogden, and Joseph Fellows. The Tonawanda Chiefs were not at the meeting and they refused to give up their territory.

Irregularities like this and the plying of Indian representatives with bribes and alcohol and ignoring the law that required Federal representation at the sale of Indian lands led to the 1922 Boylan decision. The United States Court of Appeals for the Second Circuit, in U.S. v. Boylan: 1. Denied New York State courts jurisdiction to dispose of Indian property or remove Indians without the consent of the federal government. 2. Returned a thirty-two acre parcel of land within the city of Oneida, New York. 3. Confirmed the U.S. government's right to represent the Indians as well as the state's limited authority in Indian matters.

The US Supreme court upheld the Boylan decision.

In the same month, March, of 1922 an Assemblyman from St Lawrence County, Edward A. Everett, presented the report of his New York State Indian Commission to the Assembly. The Commission had toured New York Indian reservations and studied New York Indian treaties for the previous four years. Everywhere the Commission went, Indians protested the misappropriation of their lands and made it clear they had been complaining about it for 150 years. New York State had colluded in the illegal land transfers and turned a deaf ear to the complaints. The report concluded that the Iroquois were legally in possession of the 6 million New York acres granted to them in the Treaty of Fort Stanwix in 1784.

The Everett report was rejected by the Assembly and lay buried until 1970.

Doctor Horton presented the Everett Report as evidence for how badly we had treated New York State Indians. He made this point emphatically, "Wherever the Commission went the Indians said, 'We know we've been cheated. Now leave us alone with what we have.'

"The Everett report documented that the Seneca lands had been fraudulently taken. But Everett was the only Commissioner who would sign the document and the Assembly ignored it. The report was lost except for one copy preserved by Everett's secretary Lulu Stillman. In 1980 Helen Uptman resurrected the Everett report and published it in a book along with other invaluable Seneca papers.

Horton concluded, "George Heron, a Seneca Nation President, was a good friend of mine. The little racial tensions that came up we handled well, even the brutal murder of Penny Brown." Here he referred to the murder of a popular young white Salamanca woman by a Seneca teen. The incident had the potential to trigger a violent racial outburst.

Doctor Horton gave us only a taste of this troubling subject, one to which he has devoted much of his life. He lived through the Kinzua Dam and Route 86 appropriation of Seneca lands and the negotiations over the non-Indian leases of Seneca land in the City of Salamanca. Now he is in a position to observe a renaissance of the Seneca Nation financed by self-destructive white appetites for tobacco and gaming.

We gave Doctor Horton a hardy round of applause and he fielded questions for another fifteen minutes.

TYLER HERON
AND
KINZUA RESERVOIR

From 1956 to 1965 the Seneca Nation battled for survival as the construction of the Kinzua Dam swallowed up a third of the Allegany Reservation, all of the Cornplanter Reservation and removed a hundred and fifty families from their ancestral homes. The language of the law which provided meager compensation for their losses called for the Termination of the Seneca Nation. During these horrific times George Heron served two terms as President of the Nation and led it, in the style of Cornplanter, to survival and prosperity.

Tyler Heron is a big guy, over six foot tall and 200 pounds. His size must have made him an imposing figure on the Red House football team a few years ago and more recently on the job as an Iron Worker Foreman. His manner, in speaking to the Allegany Historical Society today, however, was jovial and gentle, with flashes of smoldering anger as he talked of federal abuse of power in the Kinzua removal of the Senecas.

Tyler is in his seventies. His father, George Heron, who died at 92 in 2011, was President of the Seneca Nation from 1958 to 1960 and from 1962 to 1964. George led the Nation during those turbulent times in which the Seneca Nation fought the Kinzua Dam and fought for its own existence as a Nation. As a boy, Tyler lived on the Seneca Allegany Reservation through that epoch.

Tyler Heron

"I am Tyler Heron of the Deer Clan," he said. "My father was George. My Mother was June. He came from the Allegany Reservation. She came from Cattaraugus. He spoke nothing but Seneca till he was five years old and he went to an all-Indian school through sixth grade. He could think in Seneca.

"My father was an iron worker till 1960. Then he went back from '66 to '83. He was a regular guy, faced with a tough situation. He showed leadership and fortitude and he fought for our survival. It was a terrible time but we got through it not so bad. We've got three casinos and everyone's working.

"I have a lot of my dad's stories. I even got him on tape. The other day I was playing one of the tapes. My wife heard him. She thought we were spooked.

"He remembered old ladies' gossip. He said, 'If you want to know what's going on, listen to the old ladies. Go visit them... but don't go when there's a game show on TV.'

"He was raised by Aunt Jenny. He swore by her. If she said it, it was so. She could predict the weather. She knew about the lights on Ga'hai Hill.

"They wanted to put a communication tower up on Ga'hai. There was a public outcry. We had a big meeting. There was not going to be a tower up there. That is our place. The tower didn't go up.

"My father was an iron worker in a situation. He spoke up. He quoted the Canandaigua treaty of 1794. At Canandaigua, George Washington gave his word that the land would be ours forever.

"When Congress passed a bill to study the construction of the Kinzua Dam and confiscate our lands, President Eisenhower refused to sign it. He said, 'I won't be the first to break George Washington's word.'

"Congress overruled Eisenhower and authorized that study that led to the Kinzua Dam.

"It was the big money people from Pittsburgh who were behind the Kinzua idea. It was politics. JFK had promised to help us prevent the Dam. The Pittsburgh big money people elected him so he backed down.

"But we were sophisticated in White Man's Politics. We went to the architect who designed the Tennessee Valley Authority, Doctor Morgan. He designed an alternate plan. The Morgan Plan would have diverted flood waters into Lake Erie.

"The Army Corps of Engineers ignored it and went ahead with their own Kinzua Dam plan.

"From 1960 to '68 it was a matter of survival for us. The Federal Government took one third of our reservation by Eminent Domain. They decided the price and they took the land. The Act that appropriated the money included 'Termination' of the Seneca Nation. What will our people do? Will they ship us off to Buffalo, or what? What will happen to the Elders? They will lose everything? What about the children?

George Heron

"We hated the Army Corps of Engineers. One of our 80-year-old women chased an Army Corps agent off her land with a broom.

"We got our own law firm. They sponsored the Seneca Housing Rehabilitation Act. It helped us survive. It gave us the money to restore our communities and our homes. From the wreckage of Kinzua the Seneca Nation survived despite the Agencies of the United States.

"There was an old retired Colonel of the Corps of Engineers who wrote an editorial objecting to the role of newspapers in the delayed building of Kinzua. ' If it wasn't for the press, the Senecas would have been kicked off that land "*as a matter of routine*.""

"*As a matter of routine*," Tyler repeated that phrase with bitter emphasis.

"We took the high road. But we hated the Corps of Engineers. We spit on the Kinzua Dam. You can't get to it now. It's fenced off, for security.

"Every November 11th we have the Treaty March at Canandaigua. One year Dad was the keynote speaker. I drove him there. We went through lots of fields of corn. I said to him, "look at all the corn growing, just like us a hundred years ago.'

"Dad got them pretty stirred up. They warned me I better get him out of there. When he got back in the car, he said, "this is my last trip here.'

"Thirty years ago a film maker spent three or four years on the reservation randomly shooting black and white film. It was put together and my father narrated it. He spoke at the first showing and he broke down. I had never seen him break down. Seneca men are supposed to be strong, stoic. He was an iron worker. He could not go on. He walked off the stage. The audience was silent.

Tyler was silent for a moment, then went on, "I was sixteen, seventeen when they built the dam. I was eager for the future, looking ahead for tomorrow. But what would happen to the kids, to the elders? Now in my seventies, looking back I see how bad it was for them.

"Don't let it happen again!

"Even with the casino and all, now I realize what the Elders went through. Their hearts were broken. But as a young guy, I had the future. After Kinzua my father went back to work and I went to school for one year.

"Other guys went to work as iron workers. They came back telling big stories and driving big cars. So I quit school and went to work too. My first foreman had been my father's foreman. It was a generational thing.

"My father was away a lot. He was not much of a family man. He never came to one of my football games. We did not have a regular family life. I only got to know him as a man.

"He was in the Civilian Conservation Corps and then Okinawa as a Chief Pharmacist's Mate. He came back full of hate; that kill or be killed attitude. He didn't like the feel of it. He bathed in one of our creeks and felt all that wash away.

"We were on a big job in Buffalo. One piece, a connector, was out of place. It looked like three floors were going to collapse on us. My father calmly walked over to the connector and fixed it. That was the way he acted with Kinzua. I try to be that way. I was a foreman. Iron Work is a rough tough industry and I had to be tough too … but fair. My father was a caring person.

"Six months before he died, he started thinking and talking in Seneca again. Sometimes I had to tell him, 'Slow down so I can understand.'

"He sang a song that he said was Aunt Jenny's. I couldn't understand the words but I taped it. Maybe someone will translate it.

"I found this old Cold Spring picture of the Lacrosse team. My father was this little skinny guy. He was there with these big movie star Indians, you know with the chiseled jaws. He was a pretty good athlete, to play with these big guys.

Hugh Dunn called from the audience, "Tell us some of those Kinzua stories we used to talk about."

Tyler answered something like, "That's what I been doing. Didn't you listen?"

Then he seemed to catch Hugh's meaning and began, "Sometimes, after a few beers, the guy's would be sitting around talking. 'No Army Corps guy going to burn down my place. I'll burn it myself.' Then they went and burned their place down before the Corps got to it.

"'*Matter of routine, huh, a matter of routine*.' Sounds like Hitler, don't it? He asked us.

"That's why we have that meeting every year. There are speeches and we eat, just so we don't forget. So we don't let it happen again. We keep it peaceful. Don't want to make the headlines.

"Our kids and grandkids get educated but they know, *'Never let it happen again.'*

Kinzua Reservoir

"The school was going to take the kids on a field trip… to the Dam. To that place that hurt us so bad. I was the last to find out. I went down to that school and raised…

"There is some land in the flood plain behind the dam that doesn't get flooded. I'm going to go there and build something. What can they do but burn it down. I just want to push some buttons.

"I gave a lecture once on "Manifest Destiny" and Papal Bulls that gave the Whiteman the right to conquer us. How about if we take a flat bottom boat down the Genesee, discover Mount Morris and claim it for the Senecas?

"Russell Means, the Oglala Sioux activist for American Indian Rights came down here and took some pictures. He said, 'Anytime you need some help down here, just call.'

"The Corps of Engineers moved Cornplanter's grave. They didn't ask permission. They just did it. They claimed they were nervous about erosion of the gravesite. But they never asked.

"They never told us they were going to make electric power. We only sold them the water rights. They went ahead and built a power generating reservoir up on the hill. At the Kinzua Dam relicensing, we got a monetary settlement out of that.

"My son is into computers. He looked on Ancestry.com and he told Dad that he was the 6th great grandson of Black Snake. Dad said, 'No, that can't be so. Aunt Jenny would have told me about it.'

"My son David was going to Lamaze Classes. I mentioned it to Dad, 'What's that?' he asked.

"I said, 'That's when a husband goes to learn how to help his wife deliver a baby.'

"He said 'Why he wanna' do that? That's women's work.'

"I had a call from Randy John; he is a Professor over at St Bonaventure. He asked me if I knew anything about what happened to the plaque that used to be out in front of Veterans Park in Salamanca. It commemorated Sullivan's Punitive Expedition against the Senecas during the Revolution. I told him, 'It sleeps with the fishes.'

Then he confided to us, "Some of our men thought it wasn't appropriate in our territory.

Here Tyler switched his subject from Kinzua to older stories he had heard his father tell. Many of us have heard them from George ourselves and they are recorded elsewhere. Tyler talked about Ga'hai and its strange lights, the man whose hair turned white on Ga'hai, John Lanson who was a giant, and the Union Soldiers and their buried gold.

The audience stayed rapt, in attention into his second hour of speaking. He answered questions, reminisced and he lamented, "Before Kinzua we had an annual field day with men's' and girls' Baseball and Lacrosse. Since Kinzua we have never had them again.

He quoted one friend's recollection of the old days on the Reservation, "'I don't think guys used to wear underwear.' Tyler said I suppose that is reservation humor.

"I'll tell you about my first sex lesson. At our house we had a wood cook-stove, water came into the house by a pump. I used to like to get in behind the stove with our dog to get warm. One day the dog had a bunch of puppies with her. I asked my father, 'Where did the puppies come from?' He said, 'I didn't bring them there. It must have been the guy who brought the wood.'

Cornplanter Monument
Corydon-Riverview Cemetery

"After Dad got work as an iron worker, things got better. We got indoor plumbing. We were so pleased that the night before the plumbing was going to be hooked up we burned down our old outhouse. The plumber was delayed the next day. We had to use the neighbor's outhouse.

"They took us Indian kids up to swim in the big swimming pool. You were supposed to pass a swimming test before you got in. But we all just jumped in like we did in creeks back home. The lifeguard was pretty upset.

"Eventually they integrated all the schools up to Salamanca. The non-native kids wanted to test you at first. Once we got used to each other it was okay.

"My father was fluent in Seneca. My mother was not. I struggled with it. He was raised Christian. I am Longhouse. He said, 'You've got to believe something. People who believe nothing are the ones that cause trouble.'"

Someone in the audience asked, "When did you and your father work as an iron worker."

Tyler answered, "I worked at it from 1966 to 1999, Dad from 1946 to 1982.

He went on, "I worked on the Colden Tower. We were way up high above the valley floor and our voices carried all the way down the valley. The company got complaints about some of the language.

"You know when you are up there sometimes, you have to relieve yourself. You can't always come all the way down. You just walk to the end of a piece of iron and let fly. You yell 'Look out below' but the wind carries and it's too bad if the guy down there runs the wrong way.

Tyler switched easily back and forth between comic and deadly serious stories and then gave the serious ones a comic twist.

"The Cornplanter Reserve went to Court and got the right to sue for Oil City land. There was counterfeit money in that original deal. There is a statue of Cornplanter at the Reserve. Dad went down there to make a speech. On the way driving home he said, 'How long do you think that Statue would last if we actually brought suit for the land.'

"Cornplanter was a pragmatist. During the Revolution the Seneca's sided with the British but when he saw his side had lost he made friends with George Washington, saved our lands and advised us to adopt white man ways."

A question came from the audience, "Would the Senecas allow some scientific research into Ga'hai or the rock formations up on Old Baldy?"

Tyler replied. "Senecas prefer to leave things alone. In our culture, we believe in shape shifters. Who knows what you might come back with?

Then he added, "If you ask the Seneca Nation, they would say, 'No'

"Tell some more Seneca stories, someone prompted."

Tyler responded with this updated Seneca tale. It makes a fitting conclusion to this modern Seneca's account of his heroic father. "We were putting up steel for the new Hockey Stadium up to Buffalo. They built it too fast. They didn't dig far enough down and they didn't take time to burn any tobacco. A huge crane fell over. Fortunately, it didn't kill anyone.

"Then when they were hoisting the scoreboard into place, it crashed.

"Something was trying to come back.

"Maybe that's why the Sabres can't win.

"Maybe now they will blame Senecas.

Someone called out, "How much tobacco would you have to burn to fix that?"

Tyler responded with an aside to the audience and a chuckle, "You see how these stories grow."

From what I remember of George, he was probably looking down and chuckling, too.

Footnotes:
1. The paragraph below was taken from "Seneca Storytelling: Effect of the Kinzua Dam on Interpretations of Supernatural Stories" by Melissa Borgia in The Journal, Oral Tradition. For more information see: http://journal.oraltradition.org/files/articles/29i/05_29.1.pdf

Parker commented that the "Will-o'-the-wisp, or Ga'hai, is known as the witch's torch. It is not a spirit of the first order but merely a flying light that directs sorcerers and witches to their victims. Sometimes it guides them to the spots where they may find their charms." There is even a place near the current Seneca Allegany Territory in the Southern Tier of New York State that is known among locals as Gahaineh, or "shape-shifter."

2. Many Seneca and Mohawk men found employment in the construction industry as iron workers through The INTERNATIONAL ASSOCIATION OF BRIDGE, STRUCTURAL, ORNAMENTAL AND REINFORCING IRON WORKERS. http://www.ironworkers.org

MINNETINKA

Elizabeth Minnetinka Gassett (1661-1713) was left an orphan by the King Phillip's war of 1675. In that war, called the first Indian War, long-time-enemies, the Wampanoags and the Narragansetts, joined forces to end the steadily growing influx of colonists to New England.

Indians Attacking a Garrison House
Old Wood Engraving

During King Phillip's War, Minnetinka's Grandfather, Canochet Nanuntemo (1600-1676), was the last Great Narragansett Sachem. He and Minnetinka's father, Minnetinka Gassett (1625-1676), were killed in that war. Her mother had died earlier. The Narragansett tribe was almost wiped out.

Minnetinka was adopted by a Quaker family who called her Elizabeth. In 1678, at 17, she married John Corey, the eldest son of a large family of colonial Rhode Islanders. Elizabeth and John in turn had their own brood, from one root of which my grandmother's line sprang.

My own DNA is 10% Indian. My father's sister, Aunt Rita's, was 20% Indian. With so much genealogy available on the

Internet, it was possible for me to trace our family back to this period of clashes between races. The other 90% of my DNA includes contributions from Gramma's Pilgrim relatives and whopping portions from German and Irish relatives. The German and Irish DNA has its own endless supply of stories.

Minnetinka was a member of the hereditary ruling family of the Narragansetts. Her great, great Grandfather was Narraganset Chief, Mascus (1562-1618). Mascus was brother to Grand Canochet, Canonicus Gassett who lived from (1565 to 1647). Canonicus was ruler of the Narragansetts when the Mayflower arrived in 1620. He watched warily as his less powerful enemies, the Wampanoags allied themselves with the Pilgrims. It was the Wampanoags who celebrated the first Thanksgiving with them.

The Pilgrims aboard the Mayflower had had a long difficult voyage. They arrived to a cold New England winter for which they were not prepared. Exploring parties went ashore, found a deserted village and brought back corn and beans.

There was grumbling and discontent aboard ship while they waited for spring. The Mayflower Compact, which the Pilgrims devised during that wait, served to quiet and unify them.

John Howland 1599-1672 was a signer of the Compact. He came aboard as an indentured servant. During the crossing he fell overboard but grabbed a line and lived to become a leading citizen of Plymouth Colony. John's brother, Arthur, 1592-1675 joined him in Plymouth later as the Great Migration swelled the population of colonists. Our family traces one of its roots to Arthur Howland. I am fascinated with the realization that Gramma's DNA was represented both aboard that ship in John Howland and on shore in Canonicus.

The New England coast where the Pilgrims arrived had been heavily populated by Indians. Thousands of acres had been cleared and cultivated in corn, beans and squash. But the Indians, particularly the Pequots and Wampanoags, had been devastated by epidemics of European diseases a year or two before the Mayflower got there. The Narragansetts, however, were spared in the epidemics.

The Wampanoags, fearful of their, now more powerful, enemies, the Narragansetts, allied themselves with the Pilgrims. They fed the Pilgrims and taught them the agriculture appropriate to the harsh New England climate.

In 1622, Canonicus, backed by 5000 warriors, sent the Plymouth Pilgrims and their Wampanoag allies a war challenge, a rattlesnake skin full of arrows. The Pilgrims sent the snake skin back filled with powder and shot. Canonicus understood the message and backed down.

Roger Williams and Narragansetts
Engraved print

With time, Minnetinka's Great, Great Uncle Canonicus saw advantages in alliance with the English and before he died in 1647, he swore allegiance to their King. The peace that he established with the colonists in 1622 lasted till the King Philip's War of 1676. I have a copy of the deed he gave to Roger Williams in 1636 to build Providence Rhode Island. This was not just generosity on the part of Canonicus. It put an English settlement between him and his Wampanoag enemies.

Deed to Providence Rhode Island given to Roger Williams by Canonicus in 1636

In his advanced years Canonicus shared tribal leadership with his brother's son Miantenomi who was Minnetinka's Great Grandfather. Miantenomi was killed in 1643 leading a band of a 1000 Narragansetts against the Mohegans of Connecticut.

Diplomacy and compromise did not work for the Indians of New England. They were up against an unending tidal wave of land-hungry immigrants. The sheer number of European Colonists overwhelmed the Indians.

How much different would it have been, if in 1621 when the Pilgrims were weak and hungry, the Narragansetts and the Wampanoags had joined forces and pushed them back into the sea. In 1675 when the Wampanoag Sachem, King Phillip, brought the tribes together for an all-out war to oust the Colonists it was too late. The Colonists numbers and firearms ended that belated attempt with a terrible bloody Indian disaster.

Out of that disaster, through a mingling of Indian and English blood, grew my Grandmother Minnie Gifford's, clan, from which I am proudly descended.

So the question of stolen land is for me a family fight. I'd like to see justice done with no one else getting hurt.

TOM CAIN

Tom Cain stood silhouetted before a magnificent view of Allegany State Park's Quaker Lake. The view was through the broad windows of the great room in the brand new Quaker Lake Bath House. With a sweep of his right arm he pointed to a clearing in the forest on the mountain across the lake. "That's my Grampa, Paul Cain's, pasture," he said.

Tom Cain and Chris Babcock

The assembled members of the Allegany State Park Historical Society, which, that day, included many members and friends of the Cain and Boyer clans, did not have to crane hard to see that distinctive landmark.

Tom wore a striking raspberry-colored polo shirt and gray shorts. He is about average height, has a trim build, wears a graying crew cut and often a big grin. His voice carried well in this large room though I would not call it booming, as Bob Schmid did, in his introduction.

Pete Smallback was there. Pete and his father before him owned the former Tunesassa Indian School farm down the road from the Cain place. Pete said "I can sure picture what Paul (Cain) looked like in his younger days, Tom sure has the Grampa Cain resemblance!"

"Thanks for inviting me here," Tom began. "I am Thomas Cain. My father, Maurice Cain, was born here in Cain Hollow on a farm that is now in the bottom of this lake. I had grandparents both here in Quaker Run and in Red House, Paul and Mabel Cain here and the Boyers in Red House."

He then quickly ran through a rough Cain–Boyer genealogy and a list of Allegany friends and co-workers of which I caught only a few first names: Eddy, Sam, Mary, Darwin, Barry and many more. It would require the memory of someone who grew up here or a mind like Allegany historian Bob Schmid has to recognize all of those names and relationships. Along the way, Tom identified most of those folks he mentioned that were in the audience.

"Memories," he said, "Incredible memories, my memories of growing up are the history of Allegany State Park. We lived in East Randolph. On a typical Saturday, Mom and Dad would load me and my brothers, the six of us, into the station wagon and head for Grampa's. They wouldn't tell us which Grampa's. I always preferred Red House because Jim and Bob were there. We'd get to Steamburg and if we turned right we knew it was Quaker Run, if we went straight ahead it was Red House.

"We'd travel down State Route 280 alongside the Allegany River 3-4 miles. I was only 10 years old so Dad would never stop at Mooney's restaurant. He said it was 'too quiet.'" The audience, familiar with stories of wild times at Mooney's Bar and Grill, responded with a laugh.

"Then we'd come to the tiny town of Quaker Bridge. It was a little store, a post office and a couple of unoccupied buildings. At the store we'd pick up some things for Gramma. Across the tracks we came to Bill Smallback' s farm and then down the road a little more to Grampa's farm, a beautiful farmhouse in the incredible valley of Quaker Run. Now it's at the bottom of this lake.

Quaker Lake

"My grandparents had just one son, my dad, Maurice and they spoiled him. There are many, many stories about Maurice," Tom said.

Tom left most of those for a return engagement and went on with stories of his grandparents.

"Grampa Paul worked up in the Park. The farm was a hobby farm. He had a tractor, a team of horses and a couple of cows. He put up hay and he'd let me pour molasses over the hay out of a jug." He told about the molasses with glee, as if pouring it must have been a lot of sticky fun.

"The Allegany Historical Society website has pictures of the old place, just as I recall it. There was a vegetable garden.

You'd have to stop in the driveway and wait for the chickens to get out of the way. There was a chicken house alongside the barn. The house had a beautiful screened-in porch and a big wood–burning iron stove where Gramma kept a kettle of water hot. We six kids would pour in and take over that house. Gramma filled a bowl with hot water from the stove and lined us up to scrub all our ears. She was hard on Mom but she had no idea how much trouble it was to keep the six of us in line. Gramma would say 'Now, don't go in the barn. I don't want you up in the hay mow.' She was afraid we'd fall through the chutes. But we'd head for the hay mow and slide through the chutes.

"This wasn't Park then. The whole Kinzua Reservoir development wasn't here yet. My father was good friends with Pete and Bill Smallback. We'd go over there and watch the whole dairy farm operation. We'd go out to the back end of the Smallback place, out by their gravel pit and near the Railroad Bridge that crossed Quaker Run. My father would carry us two or three at a time out into mid river to fish for walleye and bass. Mom would be on shore with a grill and the rest of the kids, cooking dinner. I am eternally grateful to Mom and Dad for exposing us to these wonderful things.

"Grampa took us deer hunting. He knew where the old farmhouse foundations were way back up in the woods. Gramma was famous for her chicken and biscuits. She had a store of canned chicken so she could whip up a batch quick, to feed us before we left.

"The next weekend when we got to Steamburg, we'd go straight ahead to Gramma and Grampa Boyer's in Red House. In the winter, we always went straight ahead, to ski at Red House. They had the Poma lift in Big Basin. Later we used the ski jumps up behind the Administration Building.

"Grampa Boyer always had a Cadillac. It wasn't usually a new one but it was a Cadillac. We'd be running parallel to a train and he'd want to see how fast it was going. He'd point down to the speedometer at 60 or 70 miles per hour, and say, 'Haw, I can go faster than that.' "

"In those days, without any expressways, it was a 40 minute ride from Randolph to Red House. Red House Creek was our playground. It ran through Red Boyer's meadow. It was accessible, not buried in the woods, all clogged up with branches and fallen trees. The big deep pond by the bridge was our swimming pool. At 9 or 10 years old, I dove right off the top of the bridge. The pool was full of fish and crabs, big crabs, big enough to scare a 10-year-old but not scare my big brother.

"Up the road there was a big old bus to play in … until the bees chased you away. Now it's all rusted down to nothing. We dug up a bush there and planted it in our yard in memory of Red House.

"Gramma Boyer owned a grocery store. So they took some nice vacations. In 1925 she drove a Ford all the way down to Mexico. She wasn't neat but inside the store everything was neat. She rented five cabins in competition with the Park and us kids would help clean them up. The best thing was going to the icehouse in Salamanca in Dad's station wagon. There were great big chunks of ice covered with saw dust. We'd slide a chunk out onto cardboard and load it into the car. Back at the store we chipped ice to fill the old Coca Cola cooler. I wish I had that cooler today. It'd be worth a fortune. Gramma rewarded us with all kinds of ice cream and pop.

"In the winter Gramma Boyer would give the six of us a five dollar bill to go skiing. The lift ticket cost fifty cents that left two dollars for hot dogs and hot chocolate. We'd take along sandwiches, too. The Andersons were there and Hugh Dunn and lots of others.

"We used to hike with Princess, a mixed shepherd, a real 'coon dog.' We'd chase coons, never caught one, well, at least, most of them got away. We heard about slingshots that you could buy up the mountain at the Administration Building. Then we could really hunt coons.

"Grampa Boyer had a little John Boat. We'd drive over to the river and Dad would take two of us fishing out in the boat while Mom was on the bank with the other four, cooking. Then they'd trade off kids.

"After a while I could feel the tension here. The Park was expanding. Oh, I know a lot of people enjoy the Park. We still do. But my grandparents worried as they tried to figure out where they would go. They wound up in places that didn't compare with what they had here.

"Still, I always enjoyed the Park. Came over here to meet girls, went to the dances, skied and ski jumped. After high school I applied for a job in the Park. I got hired to work on a truck. Then I found out my job was on the back of the truck picking up garbage. But that wasn't so bad. We got to every camp and we met lots of young girls.

"The next summer I worked two days a week picking up garbage and the rest of the time cutting down elms. All the elms in the Park were dying. We cut it into firewood to take around to all the best girls.

"In the summer of 1973, Hugh Dunn and I and a couple other guys went into Big Basin and harvested redwood-sized hemlocks. They were marvelous trees, mature second-growth trees, two miles back in. We brought them out with a bulldozer. We filled 10 or 12 log trucks.

He stopped for a second, apparently thinking of all the past controversy over logging in the Park, and said, "Don't want to get into the politics."

"I got called back at the end of the summer to work another month in the Red House sawmill. We cut the wood there and sent it to the Quaker Carpenter Shop. They used it to make furniture and to frame cabins.

"Now I'm married to June. We've had a bunch of foster children, adopted two. We enjoy fishing the Allegany Reservoir. We use our GPS to locate the old foundations, bridge abutments, roadways and houses. That's where the fish are.

He paused and declared, "We've been blessed."

Then he went on, "My challenge to you is to share this with kids. We have lots of kids at the Randolph Children's Home, kids who don't have grandparents to bring them to the Park. Join our Mentors program and share the Park with them. Pass all this on to the future."

Tom closed with this moving challenge and we applauded roundly.

Tom Cain, whose family gave its name to Cain Hollow, is Chief Maintenance Officer at the Randolph Children's Home. https://www.randolphchildrenshome.org/

THE ATTEAS OF ATTEAVILLE

Theresa Attea came to the Historical Society today to spin stories about Atteaville. Atteaville was that fabled collection of five or six cottages strung along a half mile of Quaker Run Road where from 1939 to 1965 the Attea Family summered and thrived. The addition of Quaker Lake to the Park in 1965 radically changed the landscape and forced the Atteas to sell their land and move to New Atteaville a little way outside the Park. A rough idea of Old Atteaville's location is that it existed on present day Quaker Run Road between Cain Hollow and the Bear Ex-closure.

Theresa arrived smiling as, with youthful vigor, she drove a wheeled walker before her. She deposited an armload of ancient snapshots on the table at the front of the Quaker Lake Bathhouse Great Room, warmed herself at its fireplace and then spread out a map of Atteaville for study.

Bob Schmid introduced her as "Mother Theresa" and then she took over.

"Happy Easter and Happy Passover," she beamed at our crowd of friends, relatives and society members. "I'll tell you how it all got started. Back in the 1930s my cousin Bob had asthma. The Doctor told the family to get him out into the country. So my Uncle Bill, Milhem Attea, (Milhem is Arabic for William, so we called him Bill), Uncle Bill was on the Bishops Committee that sponsored Camp Turner here in Allegany State Park. So they sent

Cousin Bob down here, to camp. But Uncle Bill and his wife had lost several infant children and they couldn't bear to be separated from him. So Uncle Bill bought an old farmhouse on Quaker Run Road just outside the Park and they came down for the summer, too.

Theresa Attea

"My Dad found a place for us, across the road. They dug wells that struck a vein of water that had fed the school a half mile down the road. The Attea Artesian well is still here.

"Soon more of the family found or built houses close by. Laurie bought a house over in Steamburg. Laurie's father was "The crooked man who built a crooked house" the house he built was crooked, even the stairs. Uncle Joe had two kids, Uncle George had six. We had five or six houses in Atteaville and lots of kids and lots of fun summer after summer.

Milhem Attea's Cottage

"Then in 1965 they expanded the Park. The State came along with Eminent Domain and took it all, including the Towns of Quaker Bridge and Elko. They let us buy back our houses but not the land, for $100 each. We moved them a short way outside the Park to New Atteaville on Woodmancy Road in Randolph. We are still there.

"They were going to build a conduit around that artesian well of ours. I asked the engineer 'Why?' He said, 'We have to, in case we need to chlorinate the water.' I said, 'Chlorinate this water? It's been tested over and over for 25 years and it always tests 99% pure. Ridiculous.'

"We used to spend a lot of time at the old Fancher Pool. It was two and a half miles uphill to get there and we had to walk 'Groan.' It was always a dare who would jump in the pool first. It was so cold you'd come out blue with icicles hanging off of you. It was tough but we loved it. We had swimming meets, sometimes the Red House Lifeguards against the Quaker Lifeguards.

"There were kids from German Village and Buzzardvillle, which were the other cottages colonies just outside the Park, and from 'Seasonal Cabins' inside the Park: the Bollings, the Deinharts," she listed family after family, too many for me to catch the names.

Atteaville in Action

"We ran the Park. My sister Angie organized everything. She even organized the bears. We entertained at the Amphitheater. We sang and we danced.

"My sisters Angie and Rosemary were terrible drivers. They should never have been allowed on the road. One night we were up there at the dumps watching bears with Charlie John, the Park Director. On the way home Angie was driving. We were coming down the road and Old Scarface, a 700-pound-bear, stepped out of the woods right on to the road. She hit him and smashed the grill on my father's car. 'Oh, don't tell Father.'

"Some friends saved us. They had chains they hooked to the grill and they pulled it out. My Mother never noticed.

"In my family there were eleven of us brothers and sisters. We had wonderful campfires all the time and we played in the crick. It was a terrible shame that they reconfigured the crick. We swam in it constantly. We washed everything in it…but not our hair. It was too cold to wash your hair, thirty-five degrees.

"Our family business in Buffalo was located in the Niagara Frontier Food Terminal and once a week the men brought down vegetables, like crates of lettuce. They built a cold water refrigerator using the crick. The snakes loved it in there and my brothers loved snakes. I hated snakes. But they were just little garter snakes."

Pete Smallback was in the audience. His family owned the farm down the road from Atteaville at Tunesassa, the former Quaker Indian School. He raised his hand and said facetiously, "Do you, by any chance, remember going out hunting for sweet corn and getting caught?"

The crowd laughed, and Theresa for once a little flustered, answered, "We were in the cornfield and all of a sudden we look up. There is Mister Smallback with a twelve-gauge shot gun. He said, 'This is seed corn, If you had just said something, I'd have given it to you.'

"We didn't care. We were just going to roast it in a bonfire.

"Once, when one of my brothers had firecrackers that wouldn't light, he threw them in the bonfire and there was a terrific explosion. But we had wonderful parties and square dances in the big barn on Saturday night."

Here Theresa picked a picture up from the table. "This girl was a friend of mine. She came from German Village and she worked in Bob Banks store. I can't remember her name."

Several people suggested names but none rang a bell for Theresa. Her old time friend went unidentified but brought up a flood of memories about the store.

"We spent lots of time at Bob Banks store. He was such a nice congenial guy. He'd never throw us kids out. We'd spend all day reading magazines. We all worked part time there. It was a gas station. He had ice cream, model airplanes, he had everything. You learned how to pump gas and make milkshakes. Once he decided we had to make some money and he had us make the ice cream cones with just one scoop. That lasted about ten minutes.

Bob Banks Store

Bob was a wonderful guy. He lived in South Carolina and came up north every summer to run the store. The six little cottages alongside it, known as Buzzardvillle, were part of the business. It got the name, I guess, because a Buzzard once perched on top of one of the cottages.

"We always went to Father Mahoney's Sunday Mass at Camp Turner. Most Campers went there.

"My Mother made us kids pray the rosary outdoors every night. But my Sister Delores was very stubborn about it. One night, as we were out there praying, she was working on her hair. She had it all halfway pinned up and had pins all over the place.

"Mother suddenly ordered, 'Get in the house! Everyone in the house now!'

" Delores said, 'Oh Mo-ther' and she wouldn't move.

Mother said, 'There's a bear.' We all scooted inside, including Delores. But it wasn't a bear. It was dusk and a bush was moving in the wind or something.

"Then one time I came home and there was Mother, feeding a bear. A real bear. I told her, 'That's a bear. You can't feed a bear.'

"She said, 'No it's not. It's just a dog, just a big dog.'

"It was a bear.

"We could never do anything or go anywhere till we got the washing done. I had ten brothers and sisters so there was a lot of washing to do. Kids today have no idea of what doing the washing was before automatic washers and dryers. We had to drag out the old washtub, heat up the water on the stove and hang up 400 pair of socks and 200 hundred shirts, at least it seemed like that many. Now the Park bathhouses even have flush toilets...well we had flush toilets, too.

"Those kids used to get their clothes really dirty. I sent my kids to Camp Turner and when I got their pants home to wash, I'd have to beat them against the side of the house to get the mud out.

"We used to say about Allegany, 'It's far enough away to forget about your Buffalo worries but close enough so you can get back in case of an emergency.' I could make it home in an hour and a quarter but it would take me three hours to get down here, once I got done stopping at the Amish Village and what have you.

"My Brothers, Phillip and Junior, put up a corral behind our house for horses. My Father was only five-foot-six and knew nothing about horses but he insisted in getting up on one. What a sight to see him trying to make that horse go. And our little black and white mongrel dog loved the horses. He loved to roll in their manure and then he'd want to get up in my car to ride home to Buffalo.

"I have fifty-four nieces and nephews. With grandchildren there are a hundred and fifty-one of us now, too many to have all at one party. The kids are all over the country: Arizona, Phoenix… My kids bought a bench for me at the amphitheater. We used to entertain there so much.

"Oh, you can never bring Atteaville back," she sighed.

Theresa closed saying "I guess I am vintage age now. Come on up and look at these pictures."

We applauded and joined "Mother Theresa" and her niece, Laurie, to pour over maps and old snapshots of long-gone cottages, kids in swimming suits, horses grazing and lots of summer fun.

71

CARR CLAN CONCLAVE

David Carr

Bryan Carr and his dad, David, were here to give a talk on the history of the extensive Red House Valley Carr family. David is a trim energetic octogenarian with curly grey, once fiery red, hair. He was dressed in a red-plaid wool shirt tucked tightly into leather-belted slacks. Bryan is cheerful, bespectacled, a little taller than his Dad and casually dressed in a synthetic outdoor shirt, over slacks.

Bryan Carr examining a ledger from his Great Great Grandfather, Howard Carr's, Allegany River Store

Bob Schmid handled the introductions. He recalled that David and his older brother, Jim, were devoted to one another but were temperamental opposites. Jim, quiet and good humored, worked his way from Park Laborer to Allegany State Park Manager. Dave was a feisty, quick-tempered State Trooper and more recently mayor of Westfield NY. Both were accomplished ski jumpers. Jim passed away in 2010 at eighty-five.

Jim Carr

There were about forty of us gathered in the conference room at Camp Allegany. About half were Carrs and they all came to tell stories, as well as to listen to David and Bryan's stories. So rather than a lecture, we were treated to a Carr family reunion and stories bounced in from all corners of the room.

I knew Jim Carr from the Allegany Historical Society but I did not know his extended family. Keeping track of their names in this free-for-all was beyond me. My experience of it was like the time my cousin, Betty, held a Beahan-Jonas reunion in her family barn outside of Watertown. It was the first time I had met most of the family. My Dad moved to Buffalo, away from our North Country stamping ground. Though I knew a lot of family lore like the fact that three Beahan siblings married three Jonas siblings; Aunt Margaret, Uncle John and Grampa Tom married Uncle Newt, Aunt Oliva and Gramma Susan, but our connections had grown dim. Betty had to keep coaching me on names. At the Carr reunion, I was on my own so this missive should be regarded more for its flavor than accuracy.

Stephen Jr, George, Howie, Stephen, Homer, Myra, Clara Carr

There is ample precedent for Carr reunions. Bryan had the table at the front of the room filled with family photo albums.

Some of the sepia-toned, curly-edged ones had twenty or thirty Carrs lined up in rows to record their presence at the gatherings. In the front row of one, Bryan pointed to grey-bearded Stephen Carr, the first Carr to settle in Red House. He was born in 1816 and lived to 1906.

Before actually turning the floor over to David, Bob Schmid had a story. "In 1947, when David was working at Red House Beach, he was driving by and saw a couple with a baby had capsized their canoe 200 hundred yards off shore. The couple was safe but the baby was under water. David left his car and rushed to successfully rescue the baby."

David stepped forward, cleared his throat and said, "I had some throat surgery in July so my voice may go on me. I was born in the Park on the road below the Red House Dam."

He rattled off a list of names of families who lived nearby in Park employee houses, along what has now become the Park Maintenance road. Many of the names were familiar but the only one I got down was Art Roscoe. Later, I looked at the 1940 census for Red House. There were 79 families listed. Close neighbors of the Leon Carr family were those of Wilfred Carr, Deforest Fuller, William Frind, Louis Noles, Oscar Linberg and Lawrence Boyer.

David went on, "Just down the road were the 30 and 50 meter ski jumps and a little way further was the Bova downhill ski area.

"Western New York skiing got its start in Allegany.

"Three of us used to ride up the Bova rope tow and side-step down the hill to pack it down. For that, we got to ski for free. It was pretty expensive in those days, fifty cents. Then the boss built this huge roller for packing the slope. It had a handle sticking out front. You'd have to ski down holding on to the handle with this huge roller behind you. You just hoped you didn't fall and get rolled over.

"On the Ski Patrol, we'd tie an injured skier on to a toboggan and with ropes at either end we'd ski him down and hope we wouldn't fall.

"For school, We had a little one-room schoolhouse. The night before I was supposed to start school there, the Red House

School mysteriously burned down." David paused for a moment to let suspicion settle on him. We laughed and he went on.

Jim Carr

"They set up school for us in the Administration Building. The walls were kind of thin and sometimes we'd hear those administrators cussing. Loretta Kelly was the teacher and one of the Grants taught for a while.

"We were so close to the Lake, Mom kept warning me to stay away from the ice. I got so scared of the ice I thought… *it was going to come up and grab me.*

"Red House was a great place to live and to grow up. It was safe and we had a great gang of kids to play with."

Here again David listed names of the kids and again I only caught one, Art Roscoe Junior.

I mused that at the same time, in about 1939 and again in 40, my sister, my cousin and I were playing at the Buffalo Turnverein Camp just down ASP 2 a little way, at least for couple of weeks in those summers.

David went on and listed games they played, among which there was one that I had never heard of, "Annie, Annie Over." I Googled it: *ANNIE, ANNIE OVER is a nineteenth century child's game that is played over a lower building that you can throw a ball over and be able to run all the way around it. You call out Annie-Annie Over and throw the ball over the building to the kids on the other side. If they catch the ball they can sneak around the building and throw the ball at you or catch you and tag you.*

"My grandfather, Howard Carr," David said, "was a stone mason. He worked in the Park. My uncle, Howard Carr, worked there, too. So did I and my brother, Jim, and our kids. If I listed all the Carrs that worked in the Park it would fill two pages. Some are still working there."

Here a woman in the audience said, "I still work there, at least up till…" She went on to explain her circumstances.

David resumed, "Well, in 1959, I got married and moved to Westfield."

David paused and Bob Schmid prompted, "You became a New York State Trooper and you made a record ski jump."

I thought, Bob is getting good at interviewing our speakers from a seat in the audience. We should consider formalizing that role and have him sit up front with our guests, like a TV host.

David corrected Bob, "No, I fell on the outrun so it didn't count. I went back up but George had gone ahead of me way back up into the woods to get a good long run, it was cold and real icy. He flipped over and landed on his neck. Broke his neck… but he recovered, he was ok."

Here, in brief, is the history of the Allegany ski jumps constructed by the Civilian Conservation Corps: First meet-February 24, 1935; Last meet-February 3, 1979. Hill records: 50m jump, 188 feet, Franz Elsigan (Austria, 1956); 30m jump, 108 feet, George Boyer (NY, 1948).

David said, tossing a smile at Bryan, "I took my son to the 30-meter jump. He slid down it once, somehow. He said 'No, no that's enough for me.'"

David, Bob and Jim Carr 1995

With that, Bryan stepped in for a while, "This picture," he said pointing to one on the table, "is a Carr family reunion from 1907. The pictures give you an idea of family history, what people were doing back then. My great grandfather was a fiddler. There was an Allegany State Park Band he played in. Stephen Carr, born in 1816, came here from New England. One of our ancestors was the first governor of Rhode Island.

"Daniel and Howard were sons of Stephen. Howard's son, Howard Jr., was my great grandfather. Howard Jr's sons, Leon and Wilfred, were my grandfather and great uncle. Leon, Dad's father, was a Park machinist. Wilfred was a fishing and hunting guide.

"I have a couple of Howard Carr's old ledger books."

He picked up an inch-thick, heavily bound book and flicked through the pages. "He's got detailed records of everybody's grocery purchases."

David introjected. "Howard Carr kept a store on the Allegany. He supplied loggers coming down the river."

Bryan continued, "One branch of the Carrs wound up on Grand Island. Every year ten families of us would come back to the Park to play in the woods and the creeks. There is a picture of me skiing between my mother's legs on Bova. We used a rope tow then. A pair of mittens would last about two rides, till someone showed us how to protect them with pieces of rubber tire."

A question came from the audience "When were those houses, under the dam, taken down." Someone answered, "In the 70's."

Bob Schmid said, "The present day Park Maintenance road used to be the Red House Entrance Road to the Park. In 1929 before they flooded Red House Lake they moved nine houses from the lake bed down to that road to become Park workers homes. Most of the houses stood till 1975. The last three were taken down in 1990."

David said, "It must have been some job to move those houses. They had good solid basements, the doors and windows were all square. They did a good job. They must have put them up on skids and pulled them with horses or trucks. I'd have liked to see them do it. They were huge houses."

Lance Anderson spoke up from the back of the room with something like, "They moved that big barn a half mile down the road. They did it with horses and my mother drove the team. The horses were Chauncey and Roxie.

"The men put logs under the barn to roll it, then moved the logs."

David picked up his thread again, "In World War II, Dad got a different job. He and three friends had to drive quite a distance to work at the Rockwell ball bearing plant. We moved down to live in my grandfather's farmhouse, near the Bay State Bridge.

Bob Schmid reminded us that the Red House Town Hall survived until 2009 when the roof collapsed.

David said, "It had a stage at one end. We put on plays and square dances. We charged admission and the money went to the USO. Leo and Robert Remington played violins at the dances. The hall had hoops at either end. We played basketball there every night. We'd drive up to the Administration Building to play table tennis.

"There were dances in the Ad Building, too. That's when they had dorms set up. Women slept where the store is now and the men on the other side.

"My wife came down with the Girl Scouts and they stayed in the Ad Building. That's where we met."

A woman in the audience said, "There were several Carrs that spoke Seneca"

David responded with a story about one of the Seneca-speaking Carrs who said something in Seneca to an Indian friend, the friend replied, "I know you said something in Seneca but I don't know what it was. I haven't got my dictionary with me."

The woman said, "Most of the old farm people spoke Seneca, just like I did."

She continued, "When I went to Indian school, they took our language away. They wouldn't let us speak it."

Someone said, "But it's coming back now, isn't it?"

The Indian woman said, "There are classes for boys down at the Longhouse."

David said, "We used to play down there in the big open field."

She said, "The community field."

He said, "I watched with Dad. They played baseball, Lacrosse and snow snake."

Bob Schmid commented, "There were some excellent baseball teams that traveled all over, the teams and the Allegany State Park Band were always mixed: White and Seneca.

David said, "A train brought skiers down from Cleveland. A truck met them to carry their luggage; the skiers were carried in a very old bus. They stayed at the Ad Building. Some people took them in as boarders.

Someone brought up Russ Carr. Gary Lucas, of Bradford, said, "He was a boxer, wasn't he?"

David replied, "I don't think so but he used to get in a lot of fights."

Bob Schmid spoke up again, "You and your brother, Jim, were always very close."

At the mention of Jim's name one of his sons stood up to speak.

Although I knew Jim and Joyce from the Historical society, I didn't know their children, so I turned to the internet again. Jim and Joyce had three sons: Carey, Jay and Curtis, two daughters: Leslie and Andrea and several grandchildren. We didn't have a roll call so I'm not sure who was there or who spoke but there was a bunch of them.

I also learned that Jim was a Navy fighter pilot from 1946 to 50 and that he and I had crossed paths at the University of Buffalo where we were in the same class and later we were both members of the National Ski Patrol.

Jim's son said, "We lived on the Service Road from 1964 to 70. I vaguely remember Grampa's barn over in Bay State."

Another of his son's said, "I was born in '68. I skied at 2 years-old, before I could walk. I was the youngest of five. When I came along we had to move out of the house."

He mentioned that his dad worked to repair a house that had burned. He left me unsure whether the Carrs moved because they needed a bigger house or because they had a house fire.

Pointing to Judge Lance Anderson, he said "My claim to fame is that I once rode up the ski-lift on a judge's shoulders."

Lance got a laugh with, "That's why I'm so short."

The first son came back with, "Dad was a ski jumper. I learned to ski between his knees. The six of us came down to the Park for a week every summer."

Bob Schmid stepped in to introduce Daniel Carr of Rochester N.Y., "You all know Dan Carr. He is a former football player and shot putter, a big husky guy, now he is a devout minister.

Dan said, "I was born in 1953. I remember staying overnight with Great Gramma Bertha. They said, I was too young to go with the rest of them to the races. I had to stay home and sleep with Gramma. She had a pot under the bed for herself at night. But I wasn't allowed to use it. I had to go outdoors to pee. One of our aunts loved to pick mushrooms, even the ones from a cow patch. She said, 'They're washable.'"

David picked up on that. "Gramma was a baker and she was very fussy about it. When she was baking, we kids knew to park by the back door. If a cake didn't come out just right, she'd throw it out the back door.

"I had a temper and bright red hair. There were these two guys at school who would pester me till I screamed. I told Dad and he said I'd have to take care of it myself. One day I caught one of them alone. I pounded the snot out of him. They never bothered me after.

"My brother, Jim, never argued with our father. I did. One time I got so mad I balled my fist and just pulled it back a little."

David demonstrated that barely perceptible move with his fist held at the side of his leg.

"The next thing I knew, I was sitting on my butt. Dad said, 'You have to be faster than that.'

"After Jim and I got out of the service we were together all the time. Some people thought we were twins. One woman asked and Jim told her, 'Yes, we're twins, 4-year-apart twins."

Bob Schmid said, "Jim was in a motorcycle accident."

David, said, "He was riding my Harley Davidson, missed a curve and hit a car door.

One of Jim's sons mentioned that his father and his uncle David were both ski patrollers.

One of the Carr women remembered, "I broke my arm over at Holiday Valley. In the first aid station, a Ski Patroller asked me, 'Are you related to Red Carr?' I said, 'Which Red Carr do you mean.' He said, 'I don't know, but whichever one it was, he almost failed me on my Ski Patroller test.'"

One of Jim's son said, "Mom was a Buffalo girl. She met Dad when she came down to the wild Allegany country to ski. She taught at the Red House Indian School."

I went back to the internet to learn a little more about Joyce Carr and came up with this:

"Joyce Carr was a graduate of East High in Buffalo and received a Masters in Education from Buffalo State. She taught at the Red House Indian School and at Randolph Central School. She also taught Sunday school and was church librarian. She was a

member of the New York State Teachers Association, a Girl Scout troop leader and enjoyed camping, skiing and traveling."

A tearful woman's voice came from the middle of the group. All I caught was, "He died last year, he loved this place, he was full of great stories…"

She broke off and the room was quiet. She had spoken to honor one Carr but she expressed the feelings of a host of us who have loved Allegany and passed through this cherished place.

To end this, here is a proper, coming-out-swinging quote from David:

"Jim was ahead of me in school. Everything came easy to him. He was very smart. I wasn't. I had to read and read everything over and over. The teacher said to me, 'What's the matter with you? Your brother never had trouble with this.'

"I told her, 'He's smart and I'm dumb.

Get used to it!!!'"

JANICE GORDON FRANCE

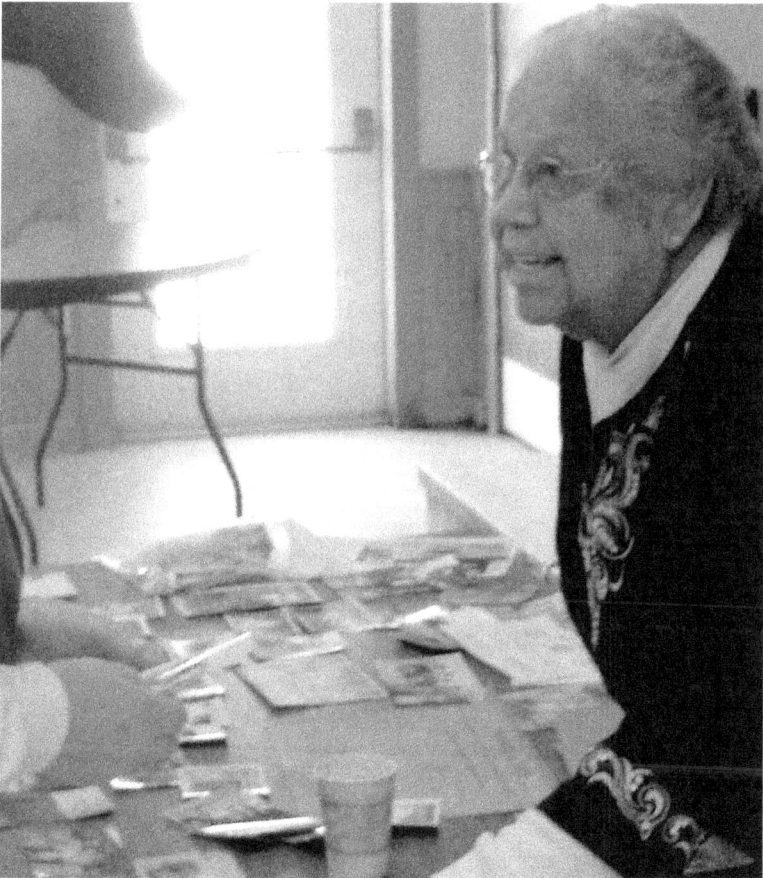

Janice Gordon France

Janice Gordon France heaped her treasure trove of photos, documents and Allegany mementos on the table at the front of the Camp Allegany classroom. Trying to arrange them in some order, she looked up at us through her rimless glasses and laughed, "Since I began this project, I need a secretary."

We, her friends, relatives and the assembled members of the Historical Society laughed with her and settled back as she began pouring out a verbal trove of Allegany history, jokes, genealogy, myths and lore.

"We are all interrelated down here, all mixed up." She illustrated this with her own background, a mix of three great Allegany families. She was born a Gordon, her mother was a Remington and she married a France. Her father was a Seneca, a fifth generation descendant of Chief Cornplanter; her mother came from white pioneer stock and she had an adopted-Seneca uncle who was a Park Ranger.

As her stories spun out, she dropped hints of her relationships to many colorful figures. But I came away hazy on her genealogy. So I reviewed my notes again, went to Bob Schmid's marvelous collection of Allegany photos and facts on the internet and then to Ancestry.com. Putting them all together I came up with the chart of Janice's family relationships which is at the end of this account.

Energetic, silver-haired Janice in her seventies wore a white turtle-neck under a black top with an Indian-looking design embroidered about the neck and cuffs. She began, "My Mother was Grace Remington, my father was Dana Gordon. We lived in Red House and my dad worked for the Park. He was too old for World War II but Evans, Wallace and Gordon, three of his brothers went off to the Army. All my Remington uncles were in WWII, the Frances were in the Air Force in Vietnam."

"School for me was way over in Steamburg. I had to catch the bus at six a.m. and didn't get back to Red House till six at night."

My Grandfather, Clarence Gordon, was a fourth generation descendant from Cornplanter. He was a surveyor for the Civilian Conservation Corps here in the Park. My father, Dana Gordon, worked for the CCC, too, and he helped build the Red House Administration Building. Times were tough, there was never enough money but we knew everyone and everyone knew us. We learned to work hard and take care of ourselves.

"Baseball was the big thing. My father pitched one famous game that was written up in the newspapers. He pitched 18 innings before the game was called with the score tied at 1 to 1, when it was too dark to see the ball. He loved the game; taught the kids to play. He loved all kinds of sports; bragged about ice skating all the way from Red House to Salamanca.

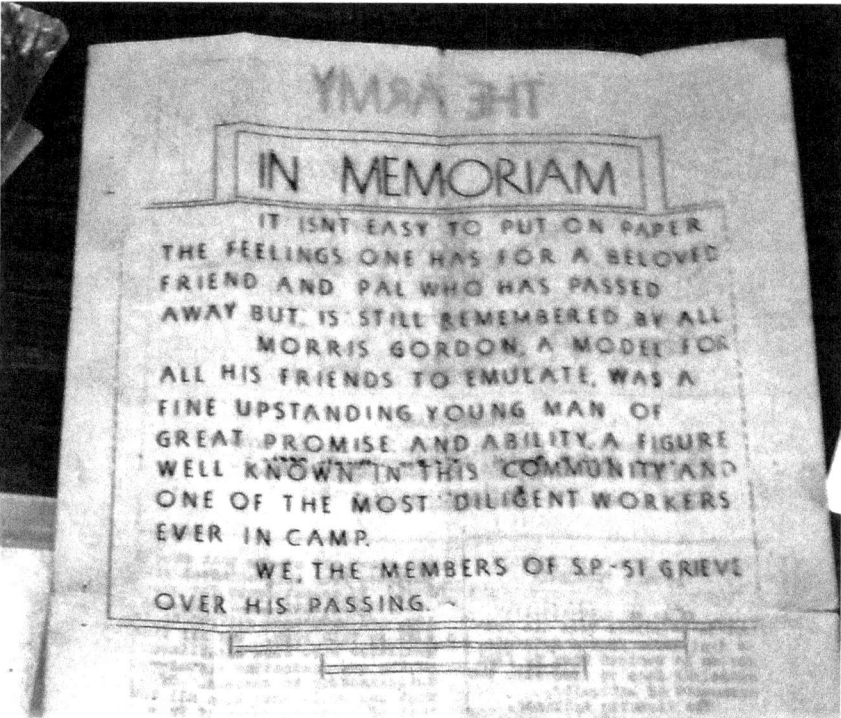

Civilian Conservation Corps
Memoriam to Morris Gordon

Janice picked up a yellowed piece of mimeographed paper from her collection on the table. Holding it up, she said, "This is a 'Memoriam' for Dad's brother Morris, published in 1933 in the newsletter of CCC State Park Camp 51. Morris was scheduled to leave, in just a few days, for spring training in Florida with the Oil City Professional Baseball team. He died in an accident while on the job with Camp 51.

"My father and his brothers loved to sing. My Grandfather, Clarence Gordon, played the piano and he could play anything by ear. Their barbershop quartet won first place at a competition down in Smithport. You remember the Mills Brothers. They were there and they wanted the Gordons to go on tour with them. But it didn't happen. You know, there were the problems with segregation.

"They used to sing in the evening at Red House. If anyone was off tune my Grandfather would just point. Anna Mae Printup and I would go out at night to listen. Exactly at 11 p.m. they'd quit.

"Sometimes we would camp out, and I mean camp out. We'd just lie down in the tall grass that had been scythed down. We'd be by someone's swimming hole. Everyone had a swimming hole. They would sing all night, under the stars. Oh, there are many stories.

"I went to work in the Park. As a young girl there I learned about snuff. I'd see men doing this sort of thing."

Here Janice made gestures with her fingers and about her nose and I think she sniffed as is done with snuff. "I figured it out when I saw this stuff fall out of their noses.

"My first job was in the Park accounting office. We worked in books on big, high ledger tables. Once I was one penny off and the boss made me work two days till I found it. And we kept those ledgers in ink.

Janice looked over at Alice Altenburg in the audience. "But there were good times, too. Right Alice?"

Alice laughed in agreement.

"When I ran the Park Concessions, Alice was one of my best waitresses. She was always right there with more coffee. Oh, I remember when we had the ski dorms in the Administration Building.

Buster France

"My husband, Buster, worked on the Bova ski hill with Hugh Dunn. I loved it because on Saturday I took the kids up there to Bova to ski and I'd have my Saturday to myself. We lived below the Dam by the ski jump. The kids were going to jump and I was worried. Buster said, 'They'll be ok.' I went out and 'Geronimo.' Then they built this big mogul at Bova and they jumped over the lunch hut.

"I ran the ski rental shop and made the chili. People didn't like the Park in winter until we had skiing. There was a Mister Chatman who hated winter but after he tried skiing he bought equipment for his whole family.

"In the summer, I thought of Allegany as a heavenly cathedral and when Labor Day came the campers would go and I was so glad. In winter I would order supplies for the concessions. There were so many wonderful people who worked for me...worked with me."

Janice picked up another ancient piece of paper from the table. "This is a certificate from the United States Postmaster General appointing my father–in–law, Neville France, Postmaster of Red House, New York the 21st day of July Nineteen Hundred and Twenty Six.

"Clayton White, according to my dad, was old when dad was young. He was one of two old men who kept the grass at the Four Corners scythed. Clayton lived by the Post Office and every day he had to make a fifteen mile-per-hour trip to pick up equipment. He let me ride with him so I gave him a cigar to thank him. In return, he gave me a card that had a dime pressed into it. A dime was a lot of money in those days.

Neville France's Appointment as
Red House Postmaster

"My father married Grace Remington. The Remingtons owned a lot of land up along Sunfish Road. My son, Todd, inherited 10 acres of it. It's good to know that some of the land will stay with the family. Mom wrote an eighty-page book describing how they lived back then. Mom and Dad joined the Indian Councilor Program. They went to Vermont to study Indian lore, how to make headdresses, proper fires and teepees. People still come to the Park and ask, 'Where are the Indians; where are the teepees?'

"Dad and his brothers worked on the Quaker dam. They called it the horseshoe dam. While they were working there a young man parked his new car on the job. The car rolled into the lake and all they could do was laugh.

"I worked for Cattaraugus County for a while; went to Albany to learn how to fill out all the forms. I got so I knew everyone in town's social security number.

"When I worked in the Park, Lynda, one of the girls, was afraid of mice so we hid a dead mouse in her drawer. We waited and waited and she didn't open the drawer all day. Finally, late in the day she opened it and she screamed so loud we were all scared. Another time we perched this stuffed hawk on the birdfeeder outside the office window. We got her that time. When she saw it she was yelling 'Hawk, hawk.'"

Bob Schmid prompted Janice from the audience. Tell us about Albert Fancher. She answered, "My grandfather, Clarence Gordon, worked in the Park as a surveyor for Fancher. He used his team of horses to move houses out from under the dam. They rolled the houses on logs. He moved big boulders and stones for the CCC and planted trees for them. The pay was a dollar a day."

Bob continued, "What about your adopted uncle?"

"Two Remington boys, Ray and Paul, were just 10 and 11 when they lost their mother. She got sick with cancer and died. The boys were split up. Paul went with another family, married had children and died in Tampa. My Great Grandfather Charlie Gordon and his wife Mary Redeye adopted Raymond Remington Gordon. They did it formally, had to go before the Council and everything. He grew up on the Cornplanter Reservation, spoke fluent Seneca and eventually married my Grandmother Gordon's sister. Ray fought in WWI and when he returned he became an Allegany State Park Ranger."

Bob interjected, "But he dropped the Gordon name?"

"Yes he did. Two names, two checks are better than one," she joked. Then she turned serious. "He was denied seniority for being a WWI Vet. He fought it to the Supreme Court and won all that back pay.

"The best chicken I ever had was down at the Cornplanter Reservation. It was frog's legs. I went down to help with the cleaning and stayed for lunch. They had gone out to get them the night before.

"In the spring we had to drink this horrible black stuff, a spring tonic. But I love fresh sassafras tea. Not the dried stuff but really fresh.

"They made spring tonics and other medicines down at Cornplanter. My father's uncles dressed up in Indian outfits and transported it up here. The women had a birth-control tea so children were spaced every three to five years.

"There was a young girl who came down to Cornplanter to stay with my Great Grandfather Charlie Gordon at the reservation. She was all bent over and weak when she arrived. He took care of her; fed her; gave her medicines. Next summer she came back, jumped out of the car standing up straight and full of pep. Her wealthy parents wanted to give Grampa Charlie money but he wouldn't take it.

Bob continued his interviewer role from the sidelines. "There were rattlesnakes up on Sunfish Road. Did you ever eat rattlesnake?"

Janice looked patiently at Bob. "No. We brought in Black Snakes to eat the rattlers. You could hear them rattling at night. It would make your hair stand up on end. They used to frighten the horses too. Once, my friend and I found a snake all coiled up. It looked like a rattler. We called the Park Police. This great big officer came over, looked at it and said, 'You know girls, I'm just as scared of them as you are.' It was just a coiled up water snake."

Bob said, "Tell us about Witches' Walk."

"My brother and I were more interested in scaring other people than we were interested in witches. We didn't live far from the Long House and we'd hear chanting there till late at night. So we put sheets and pillow cases up in trees, like ghosts. After the meeting we never heard screaming but we heard…"

Here, by tapping rapidly on the table, Janice made the sound of running feet. Then she added, "Old Baldy is considered sacred ground. The stone structures there were disturbed by archeologists. There are stories of a light coming out of the sky and of little people and spirits. Myself, I believe good spirits watch over us.

"I worked as accountant for the company that had the Park concessions. In the 80's, I was managing all the concessions for them."

FRIDAY, JULY 21, 2004 Special to The Times Herald

Reflections

Store houses memories of Red House
Dick Sandburg of Allegany shared this photo of Neville and Edna France in front of the Red House Store in Red House. The picture was taken in the early 1930s. Today this site is buried beneath the waters of Red House Lake.

Neville and Edna France in front of their Red House Store

Bob Byledbal broke in. He had had the Park concessions just before Janice took them over, "Do you know what the store Yellow Brick Road was for? It was to lead customers through the high-profit Indian souvenirs to the cigarettes, newspaper and candy in the back."

Janice said, "Yes, campers came looking for Indians. I had Indian dolls. The Park Police would shoot raccoons and I would sell the tails.

Byledbal added, "You remember we'd get the cheapest Indian dolls from Japan; open the box and they had oriental eyes."

Bob Schmid spoke up again, "Buster France was known as a master at cutting grass. He could ride that tractor across a hill at an angle where you were sure it would turn over."

Janice hadn't said very much about her husband Neville "Buster" France. That was understandable since she had just dealt with the first anniversary of his passing but he and the France family were such an important part of Park history and of Janice's life she could not leave them out.

"Same with grooming snow trails. He was an expert. He loved to be outside; Bova brings back such good memories. When he was promoted to Superintendent, he was in an office and missed the outdoors.

"You know, Buster was Red House Justice of the Peace. The Park Police would bring cases to our house at all hours of the night. I'd come to the door in bathrobe and slippers. They'd be all dressed up. They brought in one drunk who sat down at our piano and played beautifully."

Bob Byledbal broke in with, "I'll bet I'm the only one here who ever appeared before Buster as a defendant."

No one challenged Bob so he went on, "The front suspension went on my car. I crossed the center line and ran head on into a truck. The Park Policeman said, 'Do you want me to have Hook France tow your car and then you'll have to settle this with Buster France the Justice?' I looked at the officer and said Hook France, Justice France; you aren't a France too are you?

"I pled guilty and Buster let me off for five bucks."

Janice picked up her thread, "As Justice of the Peace, Buster did weddings all over; up at the Stone Tower; back at Bridal Veil Falls; over in Quaker. They'd be hippies carrying babies on their hips, all sorts of people.

"Buster and I always had someone living with us: aunts, uncles, any one down-and-out, uncle's three kids, even when we were living down in North Carolina after Buster retired, folks would come down looking for work and stay with us.

"My son was married right here in Camp Allegany. We had a pig roast; took pictures down on the lake at the point; had the reception right in this building. I did a lot of catering here. There used to be a swimming pool as part of the camp.

Janice summed up her Allegany spirit of hard work, cooperation and love of the Park with, "We held the Park employees parties here at Camp Allegany; had the annual Labor Day reunion here for 25 years. We'd hire a band for three days. The men barbecued hams and chicken, played cards all day, pinochle and euchre. We all worked together, painters, mechanics. We got along: got the job done."

Genealogy

Janice P. Gordon France, born 1940

Paternal Family

Great Grandfather, **Charlie Gordon,** 1854-1939
Cornplanter Reservation
Great Grandmother, **Rosa Lee Silverheels,** 1860-1890
third generation Cornplanter descendant
Grandfather, **Clarence Gordon,** 1885-1960
fourth generation Cornplanter descendant
Grandmother **Gertie Bell Jimeson,** 1889-1971
Father **Dana Gordon,** 1910-2004
Fifth generation Cornplanter descendant

Maternal Family

Great Grandfather **Wallace W. Remington** 1839-1912
Great Grandmother **Emma Markham** 1842-1921
Grand Father **Delbert Remington,** 1877-1943
Grandmother **Pearl R. Fahey,** 1895-1940
Mother **Grace Gertrude Remington,** 1917-1999

Husband and In-laws

Husband, **Neville Alonzo "Buster" France Jr**. 1936-2016
Father-in-law, **Neville Alonzo "Prock" France Sr**. 1896-1951

Mother-in-Law,   **Anna Margaret Bowley France** 1908-

Children

Todd France   Son
Jamie France   Adopted son
Rowdy Remington,   Guardian children
Connie Remington
Travis Remington

EAGLES
IN THE RAIN

"One Wing"

On Saturday May 23 the Park lived up to its affectionate nickname, "Cold and Rainy Allegany." Affectionate because, huddling around a wood stove, listening to rain on your cabin's roof, miles from nowhere, makes hot chocolate taste so good.

Tanya Lowe with "Merlin," a Barred Owl

On this particular day Kevin Powell, Allegany Historical Society Program Chair, had arranged for Tanya Lowe of Hawk Creek Wildlife Center to show us her predator birds and two passive-aggressive mammals, a skunk and a porcupine. A hundred and forty of us gathered in the outdoor amphitheater on the Quaker run side of the Park, probably a record for a Historical Society meeting.

Some of us took shelter with Tanya and her "critters" on the stage. Kevin and his crew rigged tent coverage over the first two rows of benches on the hill. Hot coffee, doughnuts and cookies were served to keep us warm.

Hawk Creek Wildlife Center has been an accredited Wildlife Sanctuary since 2001. They are licensed by the NY DEC and the Federal Fish and Wildlife Service. They have 80 permanent resident animals. Injured wild animals are brought to them for treatment. Those that recover are released. Those who don't recover sufficiently to make it on their own are put down or retained to perform in the center's many educational programs.

Tanya began the show with Merlin, a male Barred Owl, the Owl with the call "Who cooks for you." He was caught on the Seneca Nation where he had injured two men by diving at their faces. Normally, Barred Owls would only do this sort of thing to defend territory from other owls. But Merlin was raised with humans, so he is "imprinted" as a human instead of an Owl. He sees humans as competition and is, therefore, too dangerous to be released.

"Flint," a Male Striped Skunk

Tanya got our alert attention when she rather suddenly introduced her next performer, Flint, a male striped skunk. Nobody actually fled but I'm sure some of us were prepared to. It proved unnecessary. Flint was a quiet, affectionate fellow who let Tanya bounce him around, pet him and flap his tail. She explained that skunks are not at all aggressive but if they are frightened they will squat, raise their tail and squirt you. Since this defense doesn't work well against cars, they are often roadkill.

Tanya advised us that tomato juice will not eliminate the smell if your dog gets squirted. Pet stores do have products that work. She didn't mention it but I suspect Flint had been surgically de-smelled.

Blaze is a member of the Peregrine family, known as the fastest living creatures in the world. In a hunting swoop a Peregrine Falcon has been recorded at 242 mph. Poor Blaze broke a wing when she was hit by a car. It healed incorrectly so she cannot fly. But she has made herself useful at Hawk Creek ...as a parent.

"Blaze," a Female Peregrine Falcon

Peregrines had disappeared from NY State by 1960. With the protection of endangered species status and careful breeding programs they have begun to recover. A pair of these recovering Falcons established a nest In the Mackay Tower at the University of Buffalo where they have successfully hatched 22 chicks. Once when the tower needed repair they were put on hold, until a set of three chicks were big enough to be brought to Hawk Creek. There, Blaze took over as mother, fed them and taught them that they were Peregrines.

Alfalfa is a male porcupine from Wisconsin. Contrary to popular myth, porcupines cannot 'shoot' their quills. To get stuck with a quill you must make contact with him. Among rodents, only beavers are larger than porcupines. Old time woodsmen would never kill a porcupine because porcupines were the only creature a man lost and without food could kill without a weapon. Now humans pose their largest threat, as these animals frequently fall victim to road traffic.

"ALFALFA EINSTEIN QUILLIAM III,"
North American Porcupine

Alfalfa is a big lazy creature that spends most of his time sleeping and smells terrible. In contrast Flint, the skunk smelled sweet, while he stayed in a good mood. Alfalfa is one of the few non-predators housed at Hawk Creek, but he has over 30,000 prickly reasons why no one questions him!

The Turkey Vulture, though ugly to all but mother vultures, is a virtuous bird. He is the garbage man of the wild. He wears no feathers on his head because he sticks his head in the most disgusting places for a meal. He's not so pretty with a bare head but a lot cleaner.

Turkey vultures have a wing span of 63 to72 inches and weigh from 2 to 5 pounds. They usually have two chicks and they feed them, wouldn't you know it, by regurgitation.

Tanya kept Barf on a long tether as he obediently flew from his perch on her arm to that of the young man who assisted her.

"Barf," a Turkey Vulture

The Harris's Hawk hunts in packs; most raptors hunt alone. Harris's Hawks, natives of south western United States, are bright and sociable so they are easy to train and are often used in falconry.

This particular hawk, whose given name escapes me, put on the most complex flight demonstrations of the day. He flew back and forth between his two handlers with no tether and obligingly dodged toward and around thrilled spectators.

Harris's Hawk

A little more than halfway through the two-and-a-half hour program Tanya took a well-deserved break. She had lectured almost constantly while lugging these heavy and feisty animals around the stage.

Golden Eagle

The second half of the show was devoted to eagles. Tanya talked for a while about Eagles before bringing them out. Their nests are made of sticks and are enormous. One Bald Eagle nest was measured 25 feet in diameter and 12 feet deep and estimated to weigh 3 tons. These powerful predators, themselves, can weigh up to 15 pounds. They have a wingspread of 6 feet and talons with ten times the strength of a human hand.

Yet Eagles came near to extinction when DDT was in wide use. This chemical interfered with the formation of eagle egg shells. The delicate eggs were easily broken. Since eagles have been protected and DDT has been withdrawn from the market their numbers have rapidly increased.

One Wing, the Bald Eagle, Tanya demonstrated and who is depicted in this chapter's first photo, cannot fly. Close up his fierce eyes and savage beak are very impressive. Fortunately this huge bird's attention was not focused on us but hard on the supply of tiny dead mice Tanya fed him from a leather pouch.

Golden Eagles are common in the western United States. They have been known to knock a Big Horn Sheep off a narrow mountain perch to make a meal or two of him. Poorly sited wind turbines have killed many Golden Eagles.

Tanya completed the Hawk Creek show with the flight of the huge and powerful Golden Eagle shown abovve. He soared majestically from her to her assistant and back and landed agilely on their arms. We watched mesmerized. This fabled bird in full flight just a few feet from us made an astounding impression and an excellent finale.

We gave Tanya and the Animals a hearty round of applause and those who were sitting out in front of the stage, crowded up for a closer look.

OWLS
IN THE SUN

Hawk Creek Technician with a Barn Owl

Hawk Creek did it again. This August Tanya Lowe brought the animals and birds of Hawk Creek Rehabilitation Center to an Allegany State Park Historical Society meeting for a second stunning performance. I didn't think she could do it. They were here in 2016 and I strongly recommended that we try a different group for 2017 but it is hard to imagine that any other organization could have outshone the performance we saw this year.

The setting was perfect, on the lawn behind the beach at Quaker Lake with green mountains on all sides and the shimmering lake before us. Tom Livak and his crew provided a large tent with seating for most of the spellbound crowd of over a hundred. The weather was perfect, bright sunshine, a few fluffy clouds and, at the conclusion of the show, a dramatic thunderstorm.

Tanya Lowe at Quaker Lake

The Historical Society kids put on a simultaneous show that rivaled the creatures of Hawk Creek. As Tanya demonstrated her birds she pitched questions at three little girls in the front row. "Which bird do you think is the smartest? What do owls eat?"

One girl, the littlest of all the girls, had all the answers and looked terribly disappointed if she didn't get called on for each one. The oldest little girl put on a sophisticated above-it-all expression, another displayed her stern disapproval when Tonya said that one of the big falcons sometimes ate monkeys. Bob Schmid and his animated Grandson Louis were simply fascinated by the Bald Eagle, at close range.

"Owls should not eat Monkeys"

Tanya began with a brief description of Hawk Creek's mission. "The smallest creature we ever served was a hummingbird chick that needed to be fed every fifteen minutes. The largest was a black bear. He insisted on being fed every fifteen minutes and did a lot of damage."

The first bird she brought out was a tiny screech owl. He was molting and looked pretty scraggly. But his little ear tufts were recognizable. Tanya told us the tufts had nothing to do with hearing but helped the bird to disguise herself. "We had three hatchlings," she said. "They would perch together and each take up a different shape, one a ball, the other elongated and the third lopsided."

Tanya called our attention to the owl's huge eyes and remarkable eyesight. She asked the girls, "If you had eyes as big as hers, how big would they be?"

I don't think they came up with an answer but they looked impressed when Tonya told them, "They'd be as big as grapefruits."

She went on, "That doesn't leave much room for anything else in their heads. Do you think they are very smart?"

The girls got that right. "No."

Tonya said "That's right but even though they are little and not very smart they can take down a Blue Jay.

"The smartest bird is the crow. When I was a little girl my grandmother had a tree that was full of Japanese beetles that were being eaten by a flock of crows. The clever crows took turns, one shaking the top of the tree while the others ate the bugs that fell out. Then they would switch and another took over the shaking"

Next Tanya brought out a Barn Owl. "Not long ago, the Barn Owl was almost extinct in Western New York but they have made a remarkable recovery. That is important because one Barn Owl can eat 2000 mice in a year. Can you imagine the mice on a farm with no Barn Owls? They also eat venomous snakes. Notice their feathers are light, not so dense. A Barn Owl will land, with their wings fluffed out, near a snake. The snake strikes harmlessly at the owl's feathers and the owl twists its head around in a flash and grabs the snake just behind the head.

"His cone-shaped face contributes to his very acute hearing and vision. Experimenters once put a single candle in the middle of a football stadium and a mouse somewhere in the stands. They brought in a Barn Owl and within minutes he found the mouse."

Tanya's next bird was "Temujin," a sleek, grey-white Gyrfalcon. He was a gift from Northwoods Falconry to Hawk Creek in appreciation of Director Loretta Jones' efforts to preserve the endangered Houbara Bustard, one of the Gyrfalcon's favorite preys.

"Temujin" a Gyrfalcon

Tanya said, "His dense feathers makes him very fast, in level flight 130 mph, faster even than the Peregrine falcon we showed you last time. But the Peregrine has the speed record. In a dive it can go up to 242 miles per hour. These birds experience G forces far beyond what humans can stand.

"The Gyrfalcon is a ferocious hunter and will take on prey many times its size. A goose is too big for a Gyrfalcon to grab in its talons. So he balls the talons into fists, dives at the goose and hits him in the head knocking him out of the air."

This story brought to my mind a fabulous trip to the Antarctic that Lyn and I took several years ago. We came ashore on an island to walk among the nests of a thousand mating pairs of Penguins. We had been warned about a penguin predator, the Skua, that would see us as competitors. These big nasty birds flew at us in the fashion that Tanya described Peregrines used in attacking Geese. We swung leather camera cases in a circle around our heads and avoided the fate of the goose.

Grey Fox and Tanya

Next, for a change of pace, Tanya produced the cutest little Grey Fox you could ever imagine. She held him in her arms and petted him as she talked and he looked happy as a puppy. "His mother was injured by a car and we raised him for her. Many of you have seen Red Foxes. You remember how they would run away. Well, if you see a Grey Fox and he disappears, look up to find him. They have curved nails and can climb trees like a cat.

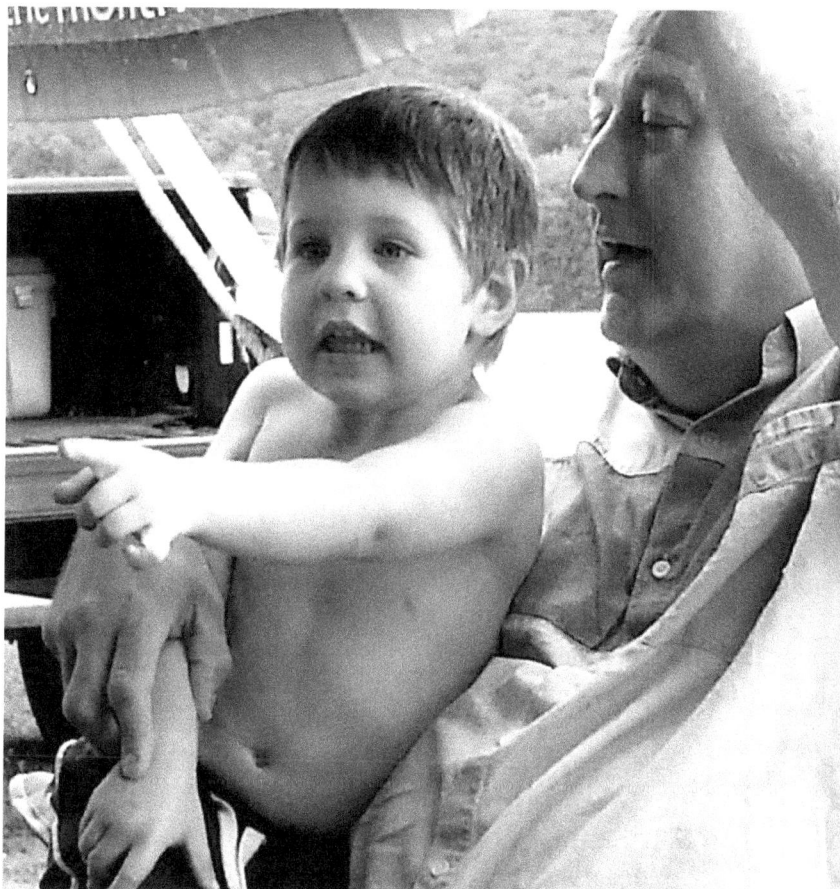

Bob Schmid and Grandson

"When a falcon attacks, he dives right on his prey. A fox has a different style. He will circle his prey and act disinterested, then suddenly attack.

Tanya gave us a few minutes for a break after her first hour. I went to the concession window at the Quaker bath house and bought one of their "small" ice cream cones. When I saw the size of the one the guy ahead of me was served, I asked if the attendant could make mine half butter-pecan and half chocolate chip and give me a cup and spoon along with the cone. She pleasantly agreed. Lyn and I split the monster and were quite satisfied.

After the break, Tanya and her assistant brought out a Red Tailed Hawk and prepared to put on a flying demonstration. She asked if there was anyone in the audience who was afraid of birds. No one admitted it. A dog in the audience was, however, asked to leave. Tanya explained that animals are wary of hawks overhead. "Once," she said I was demonstrating a buzzard or something and my boss had a sloth on the stage behind me. Does anyone think a Sloth is strong? Well, they have very powerful arms. This sloth saw the buzzard and 'went ape.' He ripped my shirt off. I made the boss buy me a new shirt."

She and her assistant wore heavy gloves for the hawk to land on and stood at opposite ends of the tent. The hawk knew that they had mice in their pockets, so he was not tempted to fly away. Tanya signaled and the hawk took off from the arm of her assistant, swooped through the crowd in the tent to land gracefully on her extended arm.

The hawk made several trips back and forth. On one of them his wing brushed Lyn's hair. She did not flinch and he did not steal her ice cream cone.

I cannot verify Lyn's story of her encounter with the hawk because I was focused intently on his landing technique. In the approach, he spread his wings to slow down, tilted his body upward in a flare for maximum air resistance and extended his talons for a precise two-point landing.

As I watched the landing, I heard, in the back of my head, my old flight instructor, Ken Angielczyk , "Ok, line up with the runway, throttle back to bleed off speed, lower the flaps another 10 degrees, pull up the nose to flare, ah touchdown, roll and… pray we don't bounce."

Tanya showed us slides of eagles, individuals, pairs and flocks of them. "Bald eagles live only in North America" she said, "so they are, appropriately, a symbol of the United States. Eagles suffered a terrible decline as a result of the insecticide, DDT. At the top of the food chain, the eagle accumulated the chemical in its body and it made the shell of their eggs very fragile. Chicks did not survive. Rachel Carson drew the world's attention to that tragedy in her landmark book, 'Silent Spring.'

"We were down to one Bald Eagle in Western New York. A hatchling was brought down from Alaska. Our lone eagle raised him and eventually mated with him. Eagles have since made a recovery so that now we can often see them around here."

At this point, Bob Schmid got up and pointed at the mountain across the lake. In his big voice he announced, "A Bald Eagle has a nest up there and you can see him fly down over the lake here almost every day!" We craned our necks, looking hopefully in that direction and remembering to keep an eye out.

Tanya completed her wonderful show with her star performers: a magnificent Bald Eagle with a 7 foot wing span and a Golden Eagle with wings that spread 8 feet.

Nature then drew the curtain for us dramatically. The sun disappeared behind darkening clouds. There was distant thunder, then lightning and soon pouring rain.

Thank You God for all your wonders.

COREY DOWDY
AND
SNOW SNAKE

Snow Snake is an Iroquois game in which teams of four, throw spear-like sticks down a raised trough of icy snow in a competition for distance. These Snow Snakes can travel a mile. The game is steeped in tradition and played with spirit.

Corey Dowdy

In the new lodge at Quaker Lake, on an overcast November Day, with the first snow of the season in the air, Corey Dowdy, an expert at the Seneca Game of Snow Snake, engaged the members of the Allegany State Park Historical Society in a conversation about this beloved Seneca tradition.

Corey is a trim middle-aged man. His long graying hair is tied back. He was dressed casually in a hooded white sweat shirt, dungarees and sneakers. He has an engaging mild manner suffused with humor but projects a deeply serious attitude about his sport. He conveyed as much in his manner, in the way he moved and the intonation of his voice as he did in direct speech.

He stood behind a table on which were displayed four long, slim Snow-Snake sticks and a bottle of dark brown Swab, the alcohol-shellac mixture that provides their base coating. Alongside him a video monitor showed us Snow Snake players in action.

Corey began, "For years I wanted to play Snow Snake."

"I threw for Dad, every single day he was out there taking care of the sticks. First he coated them with Swab, this mixture of shellac and alcohol." Corey indicated the bottle on the table. "Then he rubbed them with wax and oil in different proportions and kinds depending on the temperature and the condition of the snow. He was like a scientist, picking light weight sticks for wet snow, a heavier stick on ice. He had a whole collection of them.

"I just threw."

Listening, it took me a while to come to my understanding that when Corey spoke of "Dad" he was referring to his grandfather's Snow-Snake partner and best friend. He was not speaking of his own natural father. When I talked to him about it later he showed me a photo including his natural Grandfather, and his Snow-Snake family, "Dad," "Mom" and "Brothers."

He said, "First Grampa died, then Dad died and my brother died. Dad's sons weren't interested in playing. Would you believe it, I must have a hundred cousins and only three wanted to play Snow Snake. We four make a team and go away weekends for games." He smiled and motioned to one of them, a diffident young man in a baseball cap standing in the front corner of the room.

Seven "Sticks" and a "Mudcat"

"I'm only 50 years old but I'm grey already. My nephews are pushing me out of the way. They are making me the "Rubber." They want to throw.

"My job as Rubber is to watch the weather, decide which sticks to throw and how many coats of wax and oil go on them." Here Corey picked up two of the sticks and handed them to us in the front row. "Feel last year's varnish still on this one," he said. "And this one is bare.

"Before I start rubbing, I check the temperature and then go back and check again."

Someone in the audience commented, "You do all the work and they get all the glory."

Corey laughed, "This weekend we had a game. I tore the sticks all down and did them over. No one taught me how to do it. It is all secret. I was self-taught."

A question came from the audience. "Tell us how the game works?"

Corey said, "It's a traditional game. Whoever gets four points wins. There can be 15 teams and four snakes are thrown by each team. They used to build the track with shovels, now they use a plow on a truck. The track is about three feet high with a trough running along the top. A track could stretch from here to that blue tower." He pointed out the window to a tower in the parking lot, a considerable distance away.

He motioned toward the video monitor that showed men playing Snow Snake. Some stood in groups. One was actively pacing back and forth from the end of the track. Then he ran, stick in hand, toward it while others shouted what sounded like traditional war whoops. "This video was my first win." Corey said.

I asked "What's all the yelling?"

"They yell to distract the guy who's throwing, particularly if he's got a point." He added, "There's no swearing."

"There is 'Home advantage.' The home team can make a track to favor their own guys. A higher track is better for guys who throw overhand.

"When I was a kid, Grampa made a track for me. He made the trough about ten inches wide and ten inches deep. I said, 'Grampa, what did you use, a telephone pole?' He said it in a high-pitched kid's voice and with a sheepish grin. The audience rewarded him with a laugh.

A question came from the back row, "Where did the game originate?"

Corey answered, "It came from around here. It's our traditional game. They used to play for something valuable like a fur. They say sometimes it was used to relay messages from village to village."

Picking up a stick, he said, "You have to throw it straight. If you slap the side it will wobble." He demonstrated a wobble with his hand.

"How far can a stick travel?" a listener asked.

"It depends on the conditions. If it's icy, a mile."

"What's the record?"

"A little over a mile, by Herm Isaacs."

I asked, "How do you score?"

"The furthest throw of four gets the point."

I was still unclear about the scoring system so when I got home I took a look at the internet. Quite possibly different systems are used by different groups but here is what one source says:

A game of snow snake is played by four teams, called "corners", who compete in trying to throw their wooden "snow snakes" the farthest along a long trough, or track, of snow. The game is divided into rounds, and in a round each team gets four throws. At the end of each round, two points are awarded to the team of the person who made the farthest throw in the round, and one point is awarded for the second farthest throw. Play continues until one of the teams wins, by achieving a certain predetermined number of points

"How do you hold the stick?" was asked.

Corey said, "See that notch in the end of the stick. You hold it like this." He held it in one hand with the last joint of his middle finger folded over the notch and the stick balanced on his other fingers. It was apparent that when a player released the stick, its last contact would be that one finger joint. Noting that, someone said, "You've got to have strong fingers."

"How long are the sticks?"

Larry Beahan, Attempting Snow Snake Toss

Corey held one up, "This one is eight feet, and it's an old one. They used to say 'this one takes a man.' Today they are mostly six feet. We make them with beach, apple, ash, black walnut, only hard wood. Some use exotic woods like black ebony but that's expensive. We used to just go out into the woods and cut our own trees to make a *Gawasa,* that's their name in Seneca."

A big bearded fellow in a broad-brimmed leather hat stepped forward. "I brought several of these antique sticks from our collection at the Hanover History Center in Silver Creek. They have markings carved on them." He pointed out the markings and examined them with Corey.

When they finished, Corey commented. "I carve my grandson's name on mine."

Discussion of the making of Snow Snakes brought to mind Michael Crouse who, on another cold November day back in 2004, also spoke to the Historical Society on the game of Snow Snake.

He was a player but as a professional carpenter he specialized in making them. Here are a few notes from Mike:

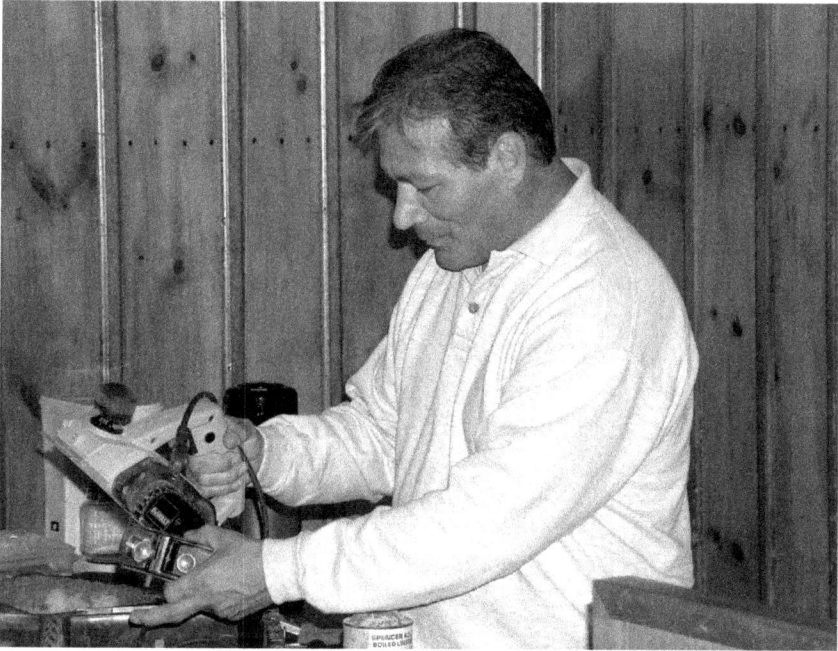

Michael Crouse, Snow Snake Maker

"We took a crosscut saw. We'd cut logs into 8-foot lengths and then into boards and then inch-square or bigger sticks. We'd take them home and use a drawknife. Mike picked up one of his snow snakes. "Make them out of Rose, Zebra, Cocobolo. Look for a pretty wood, nice grain but a wood that will work out, too. Apple is good, if you can find some long and straight enough. Hickory is long and has all the qualities you want. Maple and cherry, too. Years ago some guys colored them with food coloring.

This one is apple. Hold it one way, see the grain, another and it shifts." He demonstrated the grain of the slim, brown rod he held. He hefted the stick. "Apple is something...to work with. I picked this up the other day and it had a bow in it. It's straight today. Effected by temperature and humidity. Maple and hickory stay straight. "Every stick's a little different. You try a certain

*style. Then the wood takes over and makes it come out its own
way." Mike picked up a green-colored stick for our inspection.
With its expanded head and metal snout it looked a great deal like
a snake. "Juneberry, this one here," he said. "You look up on the
hill in spring and it is the first flowers you see. White, like
dogwood. But apple is heavy. Most are heavy. The theory is,
heavier the better."*

Corey began again, "We run tournaments for school kids.
They throw these mudcats. They are just three foot long." He
opened a blue-canvas carrying-case and demonstrated the several
mudcats it contained.

"My grandson wanted to throw, so he came along to watch
a game and stood real close to the track." Corey demonstrated his
grandson watching and head snapping to one side as an imaginary
snake whipped past."

Corey said, "I couldn't hold it against him. He said, 'Holy
shit, Grampa, that's fast.'

"It was fast.

"Don't stand close. A guy I threw for, one of his sticks
jumped out of the track. A guy was standing close to the track,
inside the roped off area. The stick went through his boot, sock and
right through his foot. The stick owner ran right over to him and
gave him hell.

"Most throw underhand, I throw side arm, some throw
overhand. We used to make a mud track to practice with in
summer, so we'd be ready."

"What do you use to polish the sticks?" The big guy with
the hat asked.

Corey looked around with mock suspicion, then smiled,
"Well, I don't think any of you are from other teams sooo... .

"It's a secret. Mixtures of muskrat oil, beaver, deer, skunk
different amounts, a drop or teaspoon. You have to be a scientist to
take it to its limits. Whatever makes the Snake fly down the track."

"Who are some of the good players?"

Corey thought a moment, modestly not mentioning himself,
"Larry Frank, George Barney."

"Can women play?"

"It's a man's sport. Women can come... if they bring food.

"It's mostly local within 300 miles Akwasasne, Mohawks, Mohicans, haven't seen Tuscaroras for a while.

"I believe we should have stuck to our ways. Women are playing now. Plastic sticks are too brittle.

"Swab", the Secret Rubbing Oil

He stopped and in an almost sacred tone said, "Wood is powerful."

"We need to keep the game traditional. It is important to us, to our background, to our tradition."

Then he returned to how the game is played. "Players are divided into First Raters, Intermediates and Beginners. But all depends on the Rubber. If they don't win they complain about the Rubber, blame it on him.

"Your own team marks the distance of your throw. You mark it with a wooden peg in the snow." He added in a serious, threatening tone, "But you better mark it carefully."

I asked, "Are there records kept of the games?"

Corey pointed to his head, "Only in here."

Then he said, "You can play the game for your life or for anything you cherish. But now you have to pay to get into the game. The winner takes the pot. I wasn't raised that way. But I love the game so I pay up.

"The first time I won, our family had just had a big dinner. Dad said, 'Ok, it's time to divide up the money.'

"I said, 'I don't want any of the money.' I talked with my brothers. We decided to keep the money in a pot to pay expenses when we travel, a room, food, entry fee.

"We won our first game the year that Dad died. He left his Snakes. My brother was dead. Mother offered the sticks to me. In Seneca culture you don't refuse anything offered to you. Even if it's their last drink, last hot dog.

"We were at the top of the hill, we won. God bless us, we won, with Dad's eight Snakes. Mom cried, happy we won with Dad's sticks. I never took off what he had put on them. There is still some of it there."

After describing this emotional scene, Corey closed our session with this announcement: "There will be a tournament in Salamanca in January or February by the old round-about in the Erie Railroad Yard."

We applauded enthusiastically, then crowded round the table for a closer look at the Snow Snakes and to press him with more questions.   Corey's nephew joined in, to demonstrate throwing technique.

ALLEGANY NORDIC

Jack Luzier

Bob Schmid introduced Jack Luzier. Jack came to Camp Allegany today to tell us about the Art Roscoe Cross Country Ski Area and the Allegany Nordic Ski Club that is based there.

Camp Allegany, where we were gathered, is located near the foot of the old Bova downhill ski slope. My wife, Lyn, and I fondly recall a ski trip to Bova in the early fifties and I have enjoyed cross country skiing in the Park many times since.

This time Lyn and I didn't ski. We came to listen to Jack, an expert, on the subject. Meanwhile, our recently retired son, Dr.

Nicholas Beahan, who came along with us, did the family's skiing. Nick skied up Patterson Trail which conveniently descends from the Summit, through the Art Roscoe system, almost to Camp Allegany's back door. He skied up and then back down to see us old folks home.

Jack began by clarifying the pronunciation of his last name for us, "In the French pronunciation the last syllable sounds like an 'A,' Luzi-aye like: the English version is 'Lose the ear.'"

That got a laugh, then he added, "I was advised to tell jokes and do a lot of laughing here since I was speaking to the Allegany Hysterical Society."

More laughs.

It may have been Rick Feuz who advised Jack, since Jack then revealed that both he and Rick had daughters who were being married this spring. He delivered this banter in a relaxed, humorous way and the audience loosened up along with him.

"I grew up in Great Valley," Jack said. "Taught Special Ed there, then went into Law and am an Assistant District Attorney for Cattaraugus County. In 2007 I moved to Humphrey NY. I have skied in Allegany State Park since 1978 or 79.

"Allegany Nordic was organized to promote skiing in Allegany State Park. The Park's Art Roscoe Ski Area provides the best double track cross country skiing in Western New York. People come to ski here from Ohio, Ontario, and Pennsylvania. We have club members from all over New York State.

"We are a 501 C3 tax free charitable organization and our volunteers collect money to provide equipment to maintain the ski trails. We have a website with updated ski condition reports so that you can find out what the trails are like before you drive 70 miles to come here and find out."

As Jack suggested I checked the website at: http://alleganynordic.org/ and here is a sample trail-conditions report:

Friday, Jan. 19, 2018 And Going Forward
Friday, Jan. 19: Grooming was done of at least the upper trails this morning; at the time I passed the distal Leonard/Ridge

junction, Ridge was not groomed past that point. The grooming greatly reduced the number of leaves in the tracks and left all three upper trails in good condition. There is no longer any water or slush on any of them. All three have some thin spots that are ski-able, or easily circumvented if you are wearing your A skis. I tried to use my waxed skis but the leaves defeated me (this was before the grooming). My 28-year-old waxless skis actually performed well. Even with the fresh grooming, the snow is pretty slick. The temp was up to 30F when I left about 12:30.

As the warming up progresses over the weekend, click on comments to leave a post of what you found. Particularly on weekends, traffic on the site runs about 150 visits a day. People who have to decide whether to drive a distance have expressed appreciation of recent reports of conditions.

19. January 2018 ***by Allen Knowles***

There followed a colorful announcement of the annual Art Roscoe Loppet on Sunday February 11, 2018. I looked up "Loppet." It is a term of Norwegian origin meaning any large long distance race, over uneven ground and usually refers to a competition on skis. I've seen a couple of them in Allegany. There are masses of competitors in 6K, 13 K and 25K divisions. They are hard work but people have a lot of fun. The theme of intense exercise is advertised in their internet address, http://heartrateup.com/

Jack continued, "The website has the history of the Art Roscoe trails and I am humbled today by the presence here of Hugh Dunn who designed these trails." Jack motioned toward Hugh, sitting at a table at the side of the room. Hugh waved and smiled. "Hughie could talk on the history of the Art Roscoe trails for days," Jack added.

"Allegany Nordic runs trail maintenance days a couple times a year. We cut back the 'face slapper' branches, repair culverts, dig ditches and identify spots for the Park crew to repair. We put up snow fences that have helped a lot to get snow cover on thin spots along the trail.

"We provide trail maps and run ski wax clinics. The Park is short of workers to groom trails so we provide volunteers who ride along with them. We organize moonlight ski events. With all that white snow and moonlight you can see very well. It is a wonderful experience." He added "We wear headlamps, too.

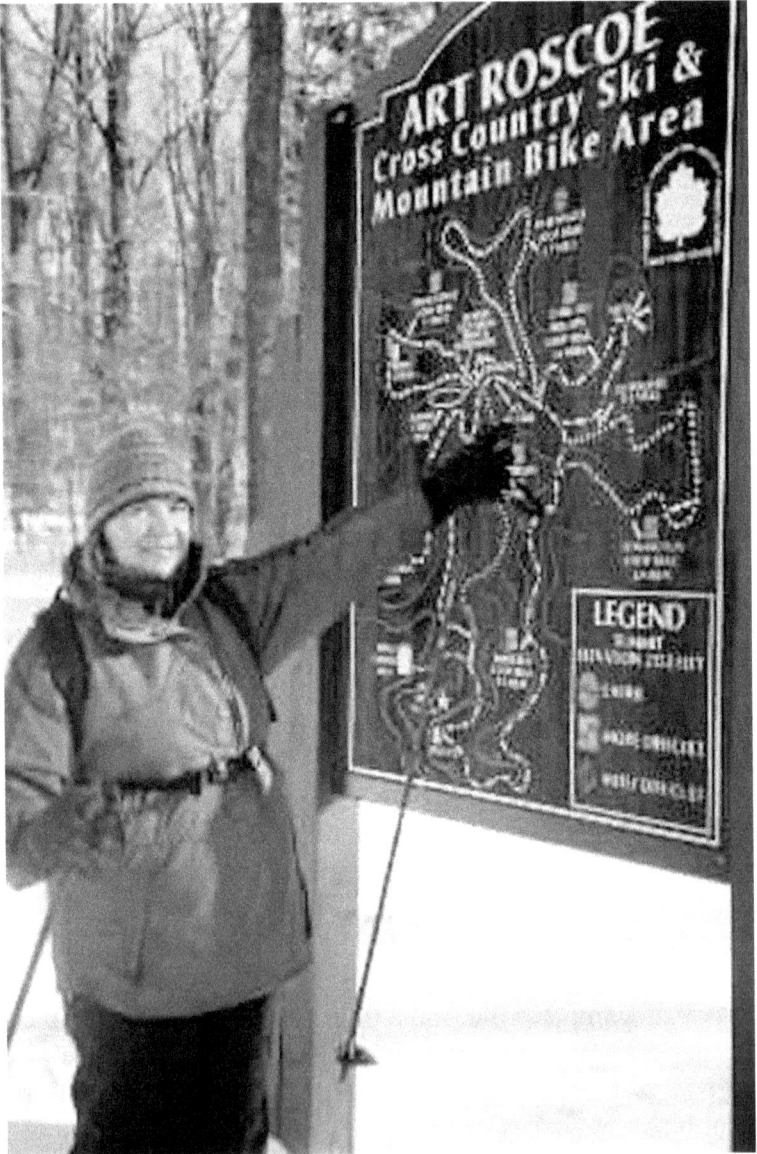

JoAnn Zurek, at the Art Roscoe X-C Ski Area

"Historically, Patterson Trail was built on the right of way of a narrow gauge railroad that ran from Bova to the Summit. It was the first trail in the Art Roscoe system. You would drive your car to the top at the Summit. Then you had a long gentle downhill slope all the way to Bova where you got a ride back up in a car."

Someone in the audience asked, "Will the lower part of Patterson be maintained this year?" Allegany State Park Manager, Tom Livak, who was also in the audience, responded, "Yes, we will do our best to groom the entire area."

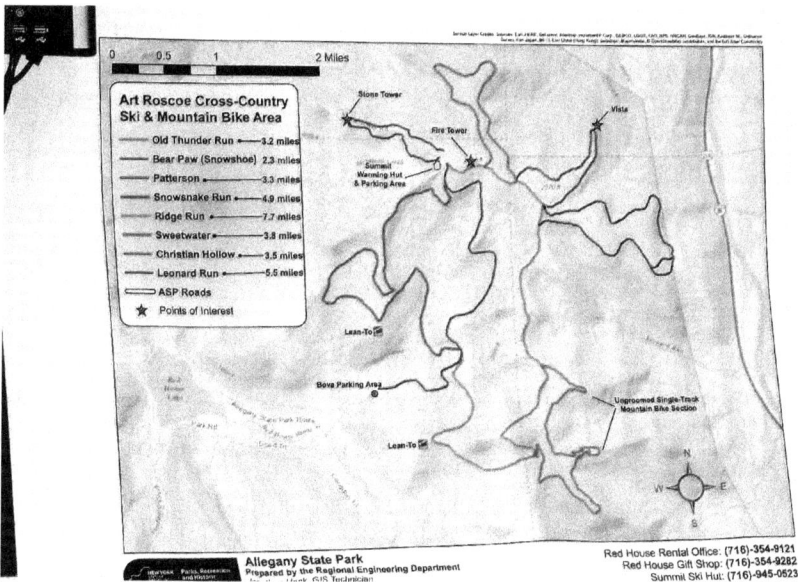

Art Roscoe Cross Country Ski Trail Map

Jack continued, "You can rent ski equipment at the Summit Warming Hut and at the Red House Administration Building. You may also be able to get snowshoes at one of them.

"There is a snowshoe trail from the warming hut over toward the stone tower. Snow Snake is the hardest ski trail. It was first designed for skate skiing. Patterson is the easiest. Having double tracks on all the trails allows for two-way traffic. Sometimes people ski side by side but that can be a problem on hills or curves when there is someone coming from the other direction. All the trails loop back to the Summit and have signs pointing to the Summit. Ridge Run follows the side of the ridge and loops back.

"The trails are used for mountain bikes in the summer. They hold the Raccoon Rally here."

I looked up Raccoon Rally and found this at: http://enchantedmountains.com/events/2017/06/annual-raccoon-rally-cycling-festival-weekend-2017-6690

Allegany State Park plays host to one of the longest standing traditions in cycling in Western New York drawing competitors from several surrounding states. The Raccoon Rally offers two days of cycling action to cyclists and families in one of the most memorable quad busting days of cycling action annually.

Jack added, "The trails are wonderful for running, too. The Park has the acreage to spread out more than private areas can. You can ski or run for miles and see no one. I don't even carry a cell phone. You know there are some of us who can recall when there were no cell phones.

"I haven't seen many injuries but there is a defibrillator available. There are lots of people out there and we have the National Ski Patrol. The Ski Patrol is a national organization that focuses on safety. Allegany Nordic is local and younger. Safety is not our mission.

"Under Tom Livak's leadership our mission of promoting skiing in the Park is almost unnecessary."

With that cue, Tom spoke briefly about the short ski season and the need to have maintenance equipment in action promptly when snow comes.

Jack continued, "We have plans to expand the warming hut and buy more grooming equipment.

Here Dan Streubel raised his hand. Jack recognized him and Dan said, "I was skiing up there once and there was a family, husband and wife and kids. They were walking carrying their skis on Ridge Run. They had left their car at Bova. They thought they were on a three mile ski and it turned into a ten mile hike."

Jack and Dan wound up agreeing that in any case it was a good idea to let someone know where you intend to go when you go off into the woods.

Dan Streubel

Jack looks very fit for a man of upper middle age. He looks like a person who exercises regularly and hard, in short he looks like an athlete. So I asked him to talk about ski racing. He picked that up enthusiastically.

"I raced when I was younger. Ski racing is different because it is a mass start with ten to a hundred skiers having to narrow down to a two-lane track and you have boards strapped to your feet. It is like the mass start in the swimming part of a triathlon. It is different, too, in that some of it is downhill like on a bike and you get a chance to catch your breath. When you run you don't get a breather. Passing is tough in ski races."

He paused and I asked, "Do you have any ski trophies?"

He answered, "Some trophies, Art Roscoe..." and left it at that.

"It is wonderful to go fast,' he said. "Like dancing on skis. When everything is right it's poetry. Like magic, the snow dampens sound in the woods. Then you hear a tree crack."

He paused and there were some questions about ski technique and waxing.

Jack stepped forward demonstrating, "Classic skiing is straight ahead with no edging, one ski forward then the other. Skate skiing is with your skis out on a diagonal. You push off their edges from one side to the other, like on ice skates.

"In Classic skiing the skis have camber. They are bent like barrel staves. When you push down on one the center portion touches the snow and is coated with either a wax that will grip the snow or a fish scale pattern that will. Grip wax goes on this center portion. Glide wax goes on the tips and tails.

"When you get it right waxing is faster. For Allegany 'Extra Blue Wax' is best. It is for twenty to thirty-two degrees. I usually use wax except when there are leaves on the trail. Leaves get stuck in the wax.

"I have seen deer on the trails, never bear or coyotes. Once I saw a tiny figure way up ahead. I got up to it and saw that it was a mouse digging a tunnel. It was funny. He would stick his head out, every once in a while, to look at me.

Jack answered a final question, "No I never ski jumped. It looks like flying, it's awesome… I'm not interested. Hiking the Art Roscoe trails though is fascinating."

Allegany Nordic

THE ALLEGANY YOU NEVER KNEW EXISTED

> *Hugh Dunn's 36 year career in Allegany State Park began in 1954. After training in Forest Management, he hired on as an Engineer Technician. He rose through the ranks to Red House Manager by 1970. From 1979 to 1990, he was Commissioner for the entire Allegany Region. In retirement, Hugh stays active in the Park as a member of the Allegany State Park Commission.*

Hugh began, "Here, for twelve years, I was at loggerheads with Sierra Club, Foothills and the Adirondack Mountain Club over our Forest Management Plan. They were preservationists; I was trained in Forest Management. It broke my heart that the Plan I worked on for so long never went into effect.

"Larry Beahan from the Adirondack Mountain Club was the first to invite me back to Allegany as a speaker and when I got done and he heard what I had to say he said, 'You are one of us.'

"Now, we are best of friends."

After that, Hugh took up *other unusual things.*

Despite a recent back injury, the eighty-nine-year-old Dunn presents as a vigorous, fireplug of a man, touched with a little sentimentality. He is as ready as ever to joke, lavish praise or go toe-to-toe with all comers and he is full of nostalgia for the old days in the Park.

"This talk," Hugh said, "is supposed to be about places in the Park you would never have expected. I sat down and started making notes." Here Hugh indicated a notebook on the table. "It's endless. It goes on and on.

Hugh Dunn

"There are at least three places in the Park that are sacred to the Senecas:

"Old Baldy is the mountain at the Red House entrance. It has ancient stone works probably built by the Mound Builders, people that were here before the Senecas. There are stories about 'The Little People' being there.

Stone Work on Old Baldy

"Witches' Walk is between the Kinzua Reservoir and I-86 just before the I-86 Bridge. It is such an evil place that, at night, only witches dare go there. The hill to the east opposite Witches' Walk is Ga-hi Hill where people have disappeared, a giant snake has been sighted and strange lights appear. Once, three Senecas traded food and clothing for a bag of gold from three Union Soldier deserters headed for Canada. The Indians buried the gold on Ga-hi Hill. No one has ever found it.

"If I was a Seneca, I would belong to the Longhouse religion. They believe everything comes from Mother Earth.

"You probably didn't know that Allegany was the third largest state park in the United States. Custer, in South Dakota, is the largest. Allegany is 10 miles square, that's a hundred square miles or 65,000 acres. In 1921, Senator Fancher and a few other influential people put up $25,000 to purchase land for a park, here.

They persuaded the New York State Governor to match it and drew a line around 65,000 acres which they gradually began to buy. Fifteen-hundred acres, inside that line, still remain in private hands.

Kids in Big Basin, Old Growth Hemlock

"Did you know that the Park had been virtually clear cut when they bought it? The Park was covered in a climax forest that was taken down in three separate cuts. All the white pine went first. Then they came for the hemlock. Hemlock bark was 8% tannin and it supported an important leather tanning industry around here. Then, finally, in World War I they cut all the rest of the timber, the beech and the ash. A chemical factory over in Rice Brook turned it all into potash and wood alcohol.

"The only Old Growth Forest left here is in the Big Basin. They left it because they didn't have the equipment to move it out. All the rest of the Allegany forest is second growth.

Gas Well, on Black Snake Trail

"How many people know that we had to let the gas company cut a 120-foot-wide, 11 mile long swath through the forest for a gas pipeline, the "K" line? It carries gas up to Buffalo and Erie County. Then in 1960 the France Brook Gas Storage area went in. It occupies 10,000 acres in the heart of the Park. In the summer they pump gas into the dome of Oriskany shale there for storage. They pump it out when it is needed in winter.

"There is oil and gas under the Park. If you go out the old Limestone Road you will pass a granite monument to Jobe Moses. In 1865, he drilled the first commercial well in New York State, at that spot, in the Park.

"Land for the Park was bought up quickly leaving 70% of the mineral rights privately owned. When we tried to buy up the rights it was impossible to calculate the value of the rights or who owned them.

"The Park administration in Albany could never grasp how Allegany's great size, its gas, its lumber and its industrial history put tremendous restraints on its management and made it a very different park. Every user of the Park wanted his use to be the primary use without thought for the others.

As if the oil and gas in the Park wasn't unusual enough, Hugh went on with the story of "Little Ireland."

"Then there is Irish Town, that settlement of Irish immigrants over near Rice Brook. Eventually, they all moved out to work in oil fields. It's heartbreaking to go over there and see tombstones for little two-year-olds who died of pneumonia. Three or four years ago, an old man who had grown up there came back to see the old place. He lay down and died. They found him a few days later.

"In 1954, I had the timber crew over in Wolf Run. There are rattlesnakes up there. One old fella named Bob lived back up in Wolf Run. He used to bring a box of rattlesnakes down to the bathing beach at Quaker Lake. I asked him, 'How can you tell if there are rattlesnakes around?' "He told me," 'You can smell 'em. They smell like cucumbers.'"

"Most people don't know that on Pine Run there was once a boarding school for black kids from the City. At Tunesassa, where the Kinzua boat launch is now, there was once a school for Seneca Indians. It was established by Quakers at the direction of George Washington after Chief Cornplanter met with Washington and asked for a school.

"NY State Historic Preservation is responsible for maintaining a lot of the character of the Park. In 1921 surplus WW I tents were installed, on wooden platforms, as the first Park accommodations. Later they built wooden cabins on the platforms to replace the tents. When we rebuilt those cabins, Historic Preservations made us build them just like they were.

Quaker Indian School

Art Roscoe

"Some of the old cabins were built up on fieldstone pillars. When we tore them down, I said, 'We can't waste that stone.' I had them dig a big hole up in Wolf Run and pushed them all in, thirteen dump-trucks full of the best Fieldstone. Then we had them to use later.

"The ski jumps were still in use when I started here. Art Roscoe built the Cross Country Skiing Trails. He was the Father of skiing in the Park and he was like a father to me."

Here, Hugh choked-up and took a breath to recover.

An important and unusual thing that Hugh deserves credit for is his management style. An important element of which was what he called "Management by walking around." On one of his meanderings he drove up on to the Ridge Road during a downpour. There he found two Park Employees hard at work, outdoors, in the rain. "Can you imagine it," he said, "two New York State employees working in the rain? I asked them their pay grade. They said GS 2. I said no it isn't. You are now GS 3."

When he directed something be done, he took responsibility for it. "We never got many complaints about the Park but once a lady came in and wanted to know 'Who's in charge?' I told her, 'I am. If there is a problem the buck stops here at my desk.'

"She said, 'There is a mouse in my cabin!' I stood up and took her hand, 'Thank God you found Elmer. We've been looking all over for him. You know, he has a wife and sixteen children to take care of. They will be so happy that you found him.'"

When Albany short-changed Allegany, Hugh went down there and fought the bureaucrats. On one trip he complained to them about the lack of staff in the Park and contrasted it with the bloated Headquarters staff. He quoted an old Seneca saying about the best way to solve a problem, "It's easier to kill a snake by cutting off its head than its tail."

When Hugh is asked why he fought so hard, he likes to refer to his compact size and say, "There is always one runt in the litter and there are only so many titties. I'm gonna' get my titty.

He took a breath and said, "Now here is something the Adirondack Mountain Club's Mister Beahan is not going to believe.

"I was totally against cutting the trees on the Red House Dam. The engineers wanted to cut them down but I knew that that earthen dam had a concrete core. A tree falling down off it was not going to take the dam out.

"Park Commissioner, Orin Lehman, listened to me and said 'Those trees won't be cut.'

Sitting in the audience, I was truly surprised to hear this revelation of a long ago conflict that we had just recently re-experienced. I suspect the rest in the room were surprised as well. During the last several months of 2016 and 2017 we had all witnessed a radical change in the appearance of Red House Dam as its beautiful cedars were stripped away. The Park explained that it was an engineering necessity. That the roots of the trees weakened this earthen dam and represented an important threat to its integrity. We had accepted that.

Not knowing who was right, Hugh or the current Park authorities, I shouted a challenge to Hugh anyway. "Let's go down to the dam and plant some cedars!"

He shouted back, "OK! I got seeds coming in the mail! See you there in April!"

That about ended the session. I went up and we shared a hearty handshake and a good laugh as I congratulated the old warrior.

Note: With the advocacy of the Adirondack Mountain Club and other preservationist groups, a new Master Plan, that protects Allegany's forest, has been implemented, a NY State Law has eliminated unclaimed mineral rights under the Park and a new gas storage lease is of shorter duration and much more restrictive.

RED HOUSE DAM

Everybody loves the cedar-lined drive across Red House Dam as you approach Allegany State Park's "Ad Building." Well, that drive is in for a haircut.

A Facebook message from Heather popped up on my cell phone. Heather belongs to "Friends of Allegany," a volunteer group that paints cabins in the Park. "Have you heard of the "improvements" along Red House Dam? It seems to have happened very quickly. I was shocked as to how far the trees coming down really are, all the way to the Maintenance Driveway, along ASP 1, towards the 4 way intersection."

Unexpected Cut on Red House Dam

I left a voice mail for Jay, an Adirondack Mountain Club friend I knew was hiking in Allegany. He answered from a mountain with good reception, "They have taken down lots of trees, a long way back from the Dam's slope. Some too big for me to put my arms around" (A tree he can't hug is big. He is six three. In Vietnam he carried the M 60 for his platoon.) "This was Northern Parula Warbler habitat," he said. "I used to show them to the Audubon Retreat birders."

I emailed an alert to friends.

Red House Dam

JoAnn, a retired school teacher, leading a Nordic Ski Club outing in the Park, texted back. "Plans are to cut from Maintenance Rd. to dam. Probably along the Lake also. There are some beautiful cedars!"

A nature writer emailed, "Sounds like the usual. Too late. You cannot re-erect a tree. But there certainly should be complaints."

An internet search produced slim information: An announcement in the Bradford Era of a project to strengthen the

Red House Dam by clearing trees and shrubs, published October 15, the day the work began. The NYS Office of Parks website had a similar announcement on October 5. A Yahoo search located an undated engineering study of Red House Dam by the McMahon & Mann firm without recomendations. Careful study of Allegany's Master Plan revealed the intention to strengthen the dam by clearing it of trees.

Red House Dam Scalped

Eliminating a forest is not an intuitive prescription for preventing erosion. But there may be less obvious considerations at play that make it appropriate to denude Red House Dam. No one is likely to argue about keeping the dam safe but an explanation of the project to the public would save a great deal of anguish and possibly legal challenges.

Park users deserve being kept in the loop, not just to avoid "Shock and Awe," but to make use of their intimate Park knowledge to accomplish Park objectives with a minimum of negative environmental impact.

NYS Office of Parks would be well advised to spend time preparing the users of the Park for changes they intend to make in such a tender and beloved place as Allegany State Park.

ALLEGANY RAILROAD RELICS

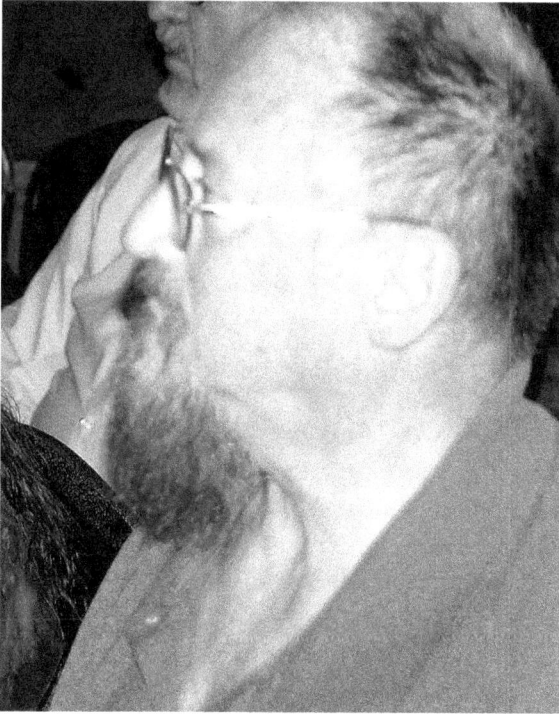

Larry Kilmer Jr.

Larry Kilmer Junior is a large, robust man. Great size has been an asset in his lifelong passion, hiking the Allegany woods and hauling out the iron remnants of its railroad past.

Referring to his size Larry said, "I'd been wanting to go back to a stretch of the Allegany and Kinzua right-of-way behind Science Lake. Dad, Hugh Dunn and I ran into a huge black bear up there. My wife worried. She didn't want me to go alone. I've seen deer and turkey but nothing dangerous. So I was up there alone, searching as usual. Then I heard this crunch-crunching. I turned around and there was this great big wolf staring at me. I know coyotes. This was a wolf, a big one. He must have been looking at the size of me and thinking, 'Hmm, that could last me over winter, till spring'"

Larry Kilmer Senior was well known as the expert on railroads in Allegany State Park. He, Larry Kilmer Jr. and William J. Fries co-authored the book, "Iron Rails in Seneca Land." Today, Larry Jr. told us of his Dad's disappointment when the book came out with authors listed: "William J. Fries" on top and under his name "Lawrence W. Kilmer and Son." "Dad said to me, 'What a shame they didn't use your name, I wouldn't have found half those railroads if it wasn't for you.'

"We used to be riding through the Park and when we found a likely spot, Dad would take a picture. I would get out and hike it. I'm not a professional at this business like Dad. There are lots of times I wish he was still alive so he could tell me how some piece of railroad iron worked.

" When we were kids my younger brother and I found an old railroad right-of-way up behind the hill in back of our house. I found a spike and picked it up to show Dad. Dad said, 'I'll give you ten cents for every one of these you bring home.' Ten cents would buy a candy bar so we went hunting. Pretty soon he said, 'Ok, that's enough.'

"The next thing I found was a small round iron ball. I thought I had found a ball-bearing off of a locomotive. Dad said, 'I don't think so. Locomotives didn't have ball-bearings.' We showed it to some Civil War Enactors . They said that it was Civil War grape shot."

"Dad and I walked the railroads all over the Park. He talked to relatives of the builder of the Patterson railroad and all sorts of people with knowledge of Park Railroad history. As a kid, I was really excited by all this history. Walking the tracks with him I'd pick up everything we found. I just couldn't leave it there to rust.

"I found a journal box cover, a brake shoe, pieces of track. People wanted the stuff. Pretty soon I got myself a cheap metal detector and began what turned into quite a collection."

Larry had laid out an extensive display of railroad iron relics on tables in front of the fireplace in the Quaker Lake great room and behind the tables he had bulletin boards covered with railroad photos and documents. There was a piece of nearly standard gauge track about eight inches long holding down a corner of a map. Off to one side he had assembled a three-foot long mockup of light-weight track nailed to four-inch timbers. Pointing to it he said, "This came from a saw mill. Sometimes over rough ground they would put tracks up on stringer rail like this. The spikes would be in at a different angle than over regular ties.

Braking Wheel

"Originally the railroads had no air brakes. Just a wheel that a brakeman would turn to tighten a brake shoe applied to one of the car wheel's tread. If the brake shoe broke there was no way to stop." On the table there was a rusted braking wheel about two feet in diameter with most of the spokes long gone.

"I'd be hiking with Dad and we'd find a journal box or piece of track. He'd take a picture and I'd pick it up. He'd say, 'What do you want with that?' I'd say, 'It's History.'

"One time I was out alone and even though I'm not supposed to carry heavy weights, I had a backpack so full of stuff that I had to roll over on my stomach and do a push-up in order to stand. Then I found this chain. I couldn't leave it. I hung it around my neck and staggered home. Dad probably rolled over in his grave."

Journal Box

Pointing to a foot square chunk of iron with the letters BNY& PRR, he said, "I found this Buffalo, New York and

Philadelphia journal box. I went to the Railroad museum and told them about it. They said, 'You're a liar. The BNY& P never used that kind of journal box.' I brought it in and showed it to them. They said, 'Well you've got the only one.'

Larry added, "There is just one picture in existence showing this style of journal box."

At this point I had to raise my hand and ask Larry, "What is a journal box? How does it work?"

He gave a short explanation, on which, the railroad expert sitting next to me expanded like this, "A railroad car rides on two assemblies called trucks. Each truck has four wheels and two axles. The weight of the car is born by a drum resting on the axle over each wheel. A journal box encloses the drum and axle-head and has a flap that allows oil to be applied to lubricate them."

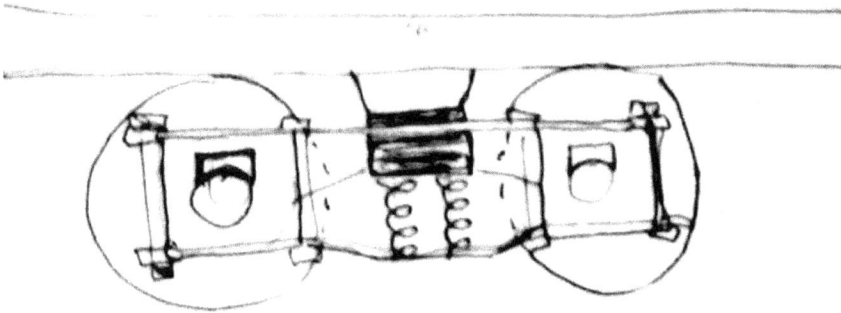

Sketch of a Railroad Car's Truck

"This friend of mine and I were in an antique store together We found a lock that looked a lot like mine. It had a key that we thought might fit it. The dealer wanted $22 for the set, which seemed like a lot of money particularly when I had no idea if it was the right key. My friend said, 'You won't be able to live with yourself if you pass this up.' So I took a chance and offered $12 for the key alone. The dealer thought twice but he took it." Larry's eyes lit up as he exclaimed, "The key fit! It worked!"

Rail Road Lock

After showing off the lock, he picked up a heavy 18-inch loop of iron and an iron rod almost as long. "This is the old link and pin coupling system that connected cars. If you weren't quick enough you lost a finger, maybe a hand or even your life. That system was outlawed in the 1880s and replaced by the modern knuckle coupler,"

Someone asked, "Did you ever find a whole truck?" He answered I've found many pieces of truck but never a whole one.

I have almost enough pieces to make one. I did find the parts of a woodstove and I put it together.

"My father and I found a full length of rail one time. I wanted it but I didn't know how to get it home. I went back when there was good packing snow on the ground, tied a rope through holes in it and man-hauled it down to my '72 Vega. It was longer then the car, stuck way out the back end. I was moving along ok with it till I slid into a ditch. A guy with a winch on his truck pulled me out, got me going.

"When Dad saw it he said, 'What the hell did you bring that home for!'

"All I could tell him was, 'It's History.'

Allegany and Kinzua Railroad "Shay" Engine

Larry did not spend much time on the documents he had on display but he did draw our attention to a railroad stock certificate on one of the bulletin boards. It had a sheaf of unclipped coupons attached. "Railroad stock was never worth much," he said "because railroads never lasted very long. To avoid liability, they were often listed under many different company names. Some did well, others did not. No one collected the dividends on this one.

"For seven or eight years now I have kept a journal of my trips and where I find things. Many of the Park roads are built on railroad grades. Dad's book is full of old maps and maps people drew for him. There are still some mistakes in it. The old railroad beds are confusing and hard to follow."

Larry has hiked so much of the Park for so long that he must be one of the best-informed, on its geography, of all Park users. Many questions were asked of him about locations of chimneys, foundations and other relics in such a wide variety of locations in the Park that I was left bewildered and wishing we were all looking at a map as he described what he had observed during his years of wandering.

Larry Kilmer Sr.
At Allegany State Park's 75ᵗʰ Anniversary

Someone asked about two old chimneys back in the woods somewhere. Larry knew the spot immediately. He identified it as the locations of blacksmith shops, one for oxen, the other for horses both located near one of the lumber camp sites. He added, "There were Irish, Italian and Sicilian logging camps. The Irish were not a problem but they had to keep the Sicilians and the Italians a mile apart to keep them from fighting."

Another audience member asked about derailments. Larry responded, "There were few reported, probably too much paper work and liability. But over near camp 12 there is a place with many, many journal boxes. There are two places near Bear Spring with journal boxes and some track. The indications were that the brakes failed and the train kept going down into the creek. There is also a story about a caboose, loaded with people, that derailed.

Larry concluded with what amounted to an invitation to visit his museum. "My father-in-law lets me use his shed for a workshop and display area. I invite people in to look over my collection. There is no charge but it is helpful to me. Visitors identify pieces for me and tell me how they work."

The audience responded with applause and by taking an advance sample of his invitation. They surrounded him and his displays, handling the artifacts and plying their collector with questions.

I'm sure that at that moment Larry Junior would have greatly valued assistance from Larry Senior who was probably looking down, eager to coach.

SING ALONG WITH SALLY MARSH

Sally Marsh and an Allegany Fan

Sally Marsh has led the Historical Society in laughing, raucous bouts of song on several occasions which I have thoroughly enjoyed. In January of 2017, her 45th year of conducting Hootenannies in the Quaker Run outdoor auditorium, she came to our meeting to tell stories of her enviable Allegany

State Park career, and not lead us in song at all. Sally surprised us. She could spellbind without music.

Lyn and I arrived to find a crowd gathering in the Camp Allegany classroom, newly decorated with curtains that Sally had instigated. There she was in a white cowboy hat and black cowboy shirt sparkling with spangles as she joyously greeted arrivals. I approached to tell her how eager I was to hear her tales and she swept me off my feet with a hug so cheerful I could barely laugh out, "Hello."

We were all impatient to get through the business meeting and on to her program but Sally did not fail us even in the business meeting. She ebulliently presented us with an idea that would fund our programs, expand our charitable reach and add excitement to our meetings: run a lottery, based on the New York Number with payouts spread across time to build tension and enthusiasm. She told stories of a gun club's great success with it and all the good that could be done with these quantities of money. She convinced almost half of us; however, the majority saw that she could probably pull this off but it would be tough going for ordinary folks like us. We decided to stick to the history business.

This did not slow Sally a whit. After a refreshment break Diane Riccardi, our President, gave her the floor and Sally, in her usual style, plunged into the middle of the crowd and took off telling stories.

I should have foreseen this. I had grabbed a front seat, early, and wound up viewing the entire show from the rear. I had no trouble hearing though. Sally's voice carries.

She began, "I grew up in Salamanca. Mom worked in the Park and I went to work with her. She had been doing bookkeeping for everybody in Salamanca. One day we were supposed to go to a wedding. It was a cold winter day and Dad, who drank too much, just didn't want to drive us there. Mom borrowed a car from a neighbor who warned us the car had no heater. There we were with presents in the back seat, me with a macaroni salad in my lap and we froze.

"Well, that did it. Mom went to work in the Park full time taking care of all their financial stuff and she bought her own car.

She invented 'flex-time.' She came and went whenever it worked for her and nobody cared because she got all the work done.

"I went along with her and got to know everyone in the Park. I loved Fancher Pool over in Quaker Run and spent lots of time there. I taught swimming in that pool for years. It was great for that because the shallow end was only three feet deep for quite a ways out, not like a lot of pools that drop right off.

Larry and Margie Beahan at Fancher Pool in 1935

"I knew from the start I wanted to be a lifeguard. When I was 17, I took the Lifeguard Test. One of the basic things you have to learn is not to let a drowning person get a hold of you. They are scared and will climb all over you to save themselves. They don't care if they drown you. If they do get their arms around you, you have to be able to break away.

"When I took the test my drowning victim was this great big tall string bean of a guy. If he got you he could climb right up you. He lunged at me and lunged at me and kept lunging at me."

Here Sally demonstrated a huge lunge with both arms in the air.

"I kept backing up till we were in the shallow part. Then I stood up and yelled at him 'It's only three feet deep. Stand up, you can't be drowning.'

"Our family could never have afforded skis for me. If it wasn't for the Interstate Ski Club, I'd never have had skis. Mom handled all their books for them. I skied at Bova and on the Poma Lift at Big Basin. The Poma was my favorite. You could meet guys. You know you'd be riding along up the hill and have a little trouble, fall off. And a guy would come and help you up …and then hang around.

"When I started college I had more time available in the summer. John Milbrandt called me in and said, 'Do you want to start working in May before the pool opens?' I said, 'Sure,' so I got to ride the garbage truck and clean cabins and do almost every dirty job in the Park.

On being questioned about it, Sally made it clear that she did not get roped into cleaning the old pit toilets.

Sally taught herself to play the Piano and the Guitar. She belonged to a Country and Western Band in Salamanca and she taught school there. She coached almost every sport the school kids played in.

After a time outdoor musical entertainment and movies became a feature on the Quaker Run side of the Park. These entertainments evolved into Sally's Hootenannies. In the beginning she distributed mimeographed song books but after all these years, the Park has supplied a screen and projector and she has a loud speaker with a cordless mike. The cordless mike allows her to roam through the audience and get even the most reticent audience member to perform for the crowd.

"You know how even if it's Waylon Jennings they are going to want him to sing his old songs. Well, they always ask me for the Ding-a-ling song. Everyone wants the Ding-a-ling song. I used to have a stick with bells on it, My Ding-a-ling Stick. One lady made a bunch of little Ding-a-ling sticks to hand out. It's all just good fun. It's like teaching kids to say "Darn" instead of…

Someone called, "Tell about the time they shut you down."

HOOTENANNY SONGBOOK

Unfortunately, I didn't catch the details of that but I think it had to do with a bunch of Boy Scouts who overdid the "Ding-a-ling" thing.

Sally introduced a couple at the front table as long-term fans that come to every Hootenanny. We applauded them. The woman sitting with them, she singled out for special praise.

"She offered to make felt blankets for raffle prizes," Sally said. "She asked me how many I needed." I said, "'Well, we have ten sessions so we need ten blankets.'

"'Fine,' she said, 'I've got twenty.'"

Raffles seem to be an important part of every Hootenanny. Sally says, "It makes people feel good to be able to help so many poor families."

It seems to me that the old truth about churches applies. If morale and attendance are down, put on a new roof that has to be paid for. They'll come back.

Sally gave the example of Gary Miller, a singer who did Elvis impersonations and had repeatedly sung for benefits for others and on stage at Hootenannies. He is ill now and Sally invited us all to a fundraiser she has organized in his honor.

One of Sally's favorite stories is about Ray Evans, a famous Hollywood song writer who came from Salamanca. He has many, many hit songs to his credit. By far his biggest hit was "Silver Bells" which is played everywhere, every Christmas, and has made him wealthy. "Once," Sally said, "I persuaded Ray Evans to come and listen to a group of kids I put together. They sang all his songs for him: "Que Sera Sera," " Mona Lisa," "Buttons and Bows." Bob Hope used "Silver Bells" in all his Christmas shows. Sally quoted Ray, 'The problem with Hope was that he didn't pay. He wouldn't pay until he needed songs for his next show.'"

Sally had great praise for some of the Park workers and Park Officials particularly John Milbrandt and Hugh Dunn. She recalled with glee how mad "Hughey Dunn" got when his surprise inspection of the Red House Life Guard room was anticipated and as he opened the door he was inundated by a pile of pots and pans.

Sally also complained freely about the lack of support she got from other Park Officials for her Hootenannies, over the years. "They sabotaged me. Two-hundred-and-fifty dollars a year was too much? Can't afford projection equipment? Once they scheduled Indian Dancers in my spot. They got 2400 protest letters saying people wanted Hootenannies. Then there was the time they scheduled me for 7 instead of 8. We got there and the place was packed waiting for me. What a cheer went up. We never got our stuff out of the car and up on the stage so quick. Going home my son said, 'Yeah Mom, but wasn't it neat the way they cheered?'

Hootenanny at the Quaker Outdoor Auditorium

"There was an older man who never missed a session. His daughter came to me and said, 'He's eighty now and can't get down to the Park. Would you like to come up to Buffalo and do a Hootenanny at his birthday party?' I said 'Sure.'

"Well, it wasn't Buffalo; it was way over on Grand Island. But we had a wonderful picnic party in his backyard. The sun shined just like it always does on Thursday in the Park. It can rain all week but when it's show time on Thursday, the sky always clears for the Hootenanny.

The crowning achievement for Sally Marsh and the Allegany Hootenannies came on August 17, 2013 when 356 voices joined to sing 14 verses of "Old McDonald Had a Farm," a feat now inscribed in the Guinness Book of Records.

So come on down to the Allegany Hootenanny and sing your heart out. Sally will be there every Thursday night at 8, from the end of June till Labor Day, to make you forget your self-consciousness and turn into a virtuoso.

Sally says "I'll be there. If I'm not, I'm just not here."

We gave her several rounds of applause. Whenever one round ended someone would pop up with another Hootenanny story and Sally would fill in the details. We could have carried on all night. Maybe some folks did.

WILD TURKEYS

Now I know where those six turkeys came from that are strutting around our neighborhood. I was amazed to see them in the heart of suburban Amherst. I had just finished cleaning up the yard, I looked out the back window, and walking across our asphalt driveway past the open garage and into our neighbor's yard was a big black female wild turkey with five eight-inch grey chicks marching in stride.

Wild Turkeys in Snyder

I live at the busy corner of Main and Darwin seventy miles from Allegany State Park. Our close-packed houses were put up in the 1930's. We expect squirrels and robins. These miniature descendants of dinosaurs were a surprise.

Tom Bergstue

In Allegany State Park, on Saturday, October 21st, 2017, I found out where those turkeys came from. Tom Bergstue, a wild-turkey field biologist who has published   many articles and videos about wild turkeys spoke to the Allegany State Park Historical Society. Tom owns a game call company and is a member of the National Wild Turkey Federation.   It was from him that I learned those five turkey chicks in my backyard are properly spoken of as "poults"… and much more turkey lore.

But inspired by Tom's talk and hints from Bob Schmid I looked into turkeys in the Park.   I talked to Hugh Dunn, a Park Commissioner, and Adele Welmann, the Park Naturalist, poked around the DEC website on turkeys and finally read several excellent articles by Bradford Era Reporter, Rick Miller.   I discovered the amazing story of Allegany State Park's role in the turkey's recovery after near extirpation from the Eastern United States.

Benjamin Franklin

Turkeys, before Europeans arrived in North America, occupied much of what is now the United States. They were a ready supply of food to the hungry settlers who swarmed across the continent shooting and eating turkeys and replacing the natural forest habitat of turkeys, with inhospitable plowed fields.

Wise old Benjamin Franklin, in a letter to his daughter regarding the proposed Seal of the United States, expressed the gratitude our young nation owed this admirable, awkward bird:

"For my own part I wish the Bald Eagle had not been chosen the Representative of our Country. He is a Bird of bad moral Character. He does not get his Living honestly. You may have seen him perched on some dead Tree near the River, where, too lazy to fish for himself, he watches the Labour of the Fishing Hawk; and when that diligent Bird has at length taken a Fish, and is bearing it to his Nest for the Support of his Mate and young Ones, the Bald Eagle pursues him and takes it from him.
With all this injustice, he is never in good case but like those among men who live by sharping & robbing he is generally
poor and often very lousy. Besides he is a rank coward: The little King Bird not bigger than a Sparrow attacks him boldly and drives him out of the district. He is therefore by no means a proper emblem for the brave and honest Cincinnati of America who have driven all the King birds from our country…

"I am on this account not displeased that the Figure is not known as a Bald Eagle, but looks more like a Turkey. For the Truth the Turkey is in Comparison a much more respectable Bird, and withal a true original Native of America… He is besides, though a little vain & silly, a Bird of Courage, and would not hesitate to attack a Grenadier of the British Guards who should presume to invade his Farm Yard with a red Coat on."

By 1840 there were no more turkeys in New York State. Eventually 75% of the state had been lumbered off. By 1900 this trend turned around. Poor producing farms were abandoned and reverted to habitat suitable for turkeys. A small population of them survived in Pennsylvania and around 1948 some moved across the border into our Southern Tier.

With good habitat available game managers tried restoring turkeys with farm turkeys raised from wild turkey eggs. These birds raised in the comfort of a farmyard lacked the skills to find food for themselves or defend themselves from predators. They failed to establish themselves.

Meanwhile some wild turkey immigrants from residual stocks in Pennsylvania established communities in New York's

Southern Tier. Officers of the NYS Department of Environmental Conservation saw this and decided to give them a helping hand. Rick Miller told that story in the Bradford Era and Olean Times Herald.

Briefly: In 1957 DEC Officer Dick Hyde came up with the idea of reintroducing turkeys to areas they once populated using a method that had worked with pheasants. The birds were trapped under nets shot from cannons and transported to new territory. He assigned a junior officer, Fred Evans, to figure out how to do it and to get the job done.

Evans persuaded Floyd Putt who owned a farm on Birch Run in Allegany NY, to let him try trapping turkeys on his property. The cannon-propelled net worked magnificently. On the first shot, Evans snagged six toms. The real snag, though, came when Evans proposed taking the turkeys off the property. Putt would not allow it.

Evans explained the trap and transfer procedure to many land owners but no one would give up their turkeys. Finally he approached Leigh Batterson, then Allegany Regional Parks Director. Batterson took it up with the Allegany State Park Commissioners and they gave their permission. The vote was eleven to one.

In March 1959 Evans completed the first trap and transfer of wild turkeys from Allegany State Park. A little way down France Brook Road, using the cannon-fired net he snared ten turkeys. He sent two toms and three hens to Cooper Hill in nearby Humphrey NY. With that the long and successful trap and transfer program began.

Officer Fred Evans gives Allegany State Park credit for repopulating the Northeastern United States with wild turkeys. No one else would give up their turkeys for trap and transfer.

Several days after the Historical Society meeting, I talked to Hugh Dunn who, back in the 1950s and 60s working in the Park Engineering Department, was part of this operation. Hugh gives the credit for the success of the program to Fred Evans, himself, for his dedication and persistence. Hugh added the fact that Evans was an amateur pilot with a plane of his own. Evans made many of the transfer runs in his plane, crammed with crated turkeys.

Hugh Dunn

Hugh said, "Leigh Batterson let me and some of the other Park employees help Evans with the nets and cannons. We did it in the winter when food was scarce for turkeys. We put corn out on one of the cabin trails. When the turkeys got used to eating there, we set up the cannon and net and waited inside one of the cabins. Ten or fifteen of them would collect there, peacefully eating our corn.

(Facing Page)

"Ad Building" Diorama of Turkey Netting

185

Display is Under Construction

We'd fire the cannon. They'd get pretty scared with the net over them. Some would lose a few feathers. We'd all run out of the cabin and calm them down. We'd crate about half of them and ship them off all over New York State. Eventually we stocked the whole Northeast; Vermont, Massachusetts, New Hampshire, Jersey, even Ontario. "The Park went all out and did a great job on the historic exhibit in the Red House Administration building."

I agreed with Hugh. The diorama shows an Allegany forest scene with four turkeys minding their own business as a net sprouts into the air over them from the mouth of something that looks like a military mortar. I mentioned that the display contained a photograph of the first successful attempt at trapping turkeys in the Park.

Hugh said, "Yes, I was looking at that and I recognized a guy I used to hunt with. I was with him during the first New York State turkey hunting season, when he got the first turkey.

"I'm not sure where the turkeys that came into the Park were from, Hugh said, but in four or five years after they got there, they mushroomed. This year the numbers are down some. The hunting season is cut to just one week. The DEC says it's fishers. They eat the eggs and climb trees at night to kill turkeys while they're roosting.

Hugh said, "I love to call them. There are 30 turkeys in my backyard right now. I've lost my will to kill. I just like to watch them."

The New York State Department of Environmental Conservation website says, "Since the first turkeys were trapped in Allegany State Park in 1959, approximately 1,400 birds have been moved within New York State. These 1,400 birds have successfully reestablished wild populations statewide. Today, numbers have increased dramatically to an estimated 250,000 to 300,000 birds."

So, that is how those Allegany wild turkeys arrived in our suburban backyard just short of Thanksgiving this year.

With all this story in the background, Tom Bergstue, our Historical Society speaker found an eager audience for his presentation of the biology of these birds. Tom wore a smile and a felt hat with a big turkey feather stuck in the band. On the tables lining the walls of the Great Room at Quaker Lake he had arrayed a mounted Tom Turkey, the turkey's arch rival the vicious little Fisher, tail feathers and spurs from prize turkeys, hunting trophy photos, a camouflage feathery hat and jacket and many, many turkey calling devices.

What struck me most from Tom's talk was his revelation of the complexity of turkey language. It is not a simple gobble. It is a collection of gobbles, yelps, clicks, clucks and purrs which employ rhythm and context in creating meaning. He made it clear that if you sit in the woods calling turkeys and put your turkey calls together in the wrong syntax, turkeys will understand that something is wrong and be gone instantly.

Some animals like deer, will come back to check it out when they are scared off but not turkeys. They are gone. They run twenty-five miles-per-hour, fly fifty-five and have exquisitely good hearing and vision. You cannot sneak up on a turkey and if you spook him, forget about it. He made it clear that this was wild turkeys he was talking about. Domestic turkeys are a different breed and nowhere near as smart.

Tom took us through a day with a flock of turkeys talking. "There are always crows around so the first thing you hear is, likely, a crow. A tom turkey may gobble back or possibly a barn owl will give his 'who cooks for you'. Barn owls and turkeys do not get along well and the tom will certainly answer. You can try one of these two calls and if a tom calls back, just sit still and he may come in to investigate.

"A female turkey wakes up on her perch in a tree, stretches and makes a few clucks, like 'where is everyone, we all came up here together last night?' Then she kind of awkwardly jumps down out of the tree and you can imitate her wing sound, brushing feathers against your shirt."

Tom demonstrated this sound with a handful of turkey feathers.

"Then a few more clucks and a purr as other females join her. And maybe a gobbler calls in with 'Hey there are hens in the area,' a deep harsh rasp almost like a beagle. Pretty quick they all come down out of the tree. There's a lot of talk and everything is ok."

Tom demonstrates this with lively gobbles and clucks and brushing of feathers. It's almost like we are witnessing a Sunday brunch for turkeys.

"But if there is a fox or an owl or a hawk in the area, there is a sharp loud rhythmic click and everyone is gone."

Tom falls silent and the turkeys seem truly departed.

He had much more to say but for the full turkey story straight from Tom take a look at his website: http://mountaincabinoutdoors.com/author/mountaincabin/

To mark the achievement of restocking the wild turkey to the Northeastern United States, Allegany State Park and the National Wild Turkey Federation constructed a stone monument just off France Brook Road. Park mason, Randy Sipko, and his assistant, James Clement, did the actual work. The monument was completed in 2016. The wording on its plaque is:

"Site of the first Wild Turkey Trap and Transfer Program. (Then the image of a turkey) Allegany State Park. Founding site for the NYS Conservation Dept. Wild Turkey Trap and Transfer Program. Birds trapped at this site helped reintroduce the Eastern Wild Turkey to the Northeastern U.S. and Southeastern Canada. 1959."

Lyn and I haven't seen the monument yet but next time we are in the Park we will take a look. It will give us a chance to reminisce about the summer of 1953 when we spent our honeymoon as camp counselors at Camp 12, which was then "Camp Arrowhead."

And I will have the further opportunity to remember the summers of 1939 and 40 when my sister, Marj, and cousin, Art were campers at Camp 12, then the "Buffalo Turnverein Camp." Art's aunt was the cook and kept an eye on us kids. One weekend, she roasted turkeys for the parents coming to visit. I recall the delicious chunks of white meat floating in tomato-onion sauce that she served us as turkey goulash on Monday. That is my fondest memory of turkey in Allegany State Park.

Monument to Wild Turkey Restoration Pioneered in Allegany State Park

250 MILES OF TRAILS

Patrick Dove, our speaker, was introduced by Bob Schmid as "The Allegany State Park Trails Manager and Development Coordinator and a super, super nice guy."

Patrick Dove

Patrick is an athletic young man dressed in a grey New York State Parks sweatshirt and a baseball cap. He wears sunglasses perched on the visor of his cap. He began, "I have worked for the Park for ten years. For the last year I have been in charge of trail maintenance …and tasked with building new trails."

On June 30, 2010 a new Master Plan went into effect for Allegany State Park. Through the magic of the internet you can read the Trail section of that plan by Googling:

Allegany State Park Final Master Plan/FEIS: Appendix B – Final Trails Plan.

The following quote, abstracted from the plan's last page, summarizes the condition of Park trails:

"In general, trails throughout the park are in need of maintenance. Many trails have trees and branches blocking the route in multiple locations and excessive brush along the treadway. There are also significant areas of saturated tread and erosion due to improper trail alignment or a deficient or insufficiently maintained infrastructure to remove water from the trail surface, including blocked culverts. …… park trails are generally deficient in adequate signage and waymarks, and enforcement is needed to protect against unauthorized uses of trails. Many trailheads that have existing signs are in need of updated and/or improved signage."

So Patrick is the guy with the job of fixing the myriad trail problems described in the Trail Master Plan.

Before getting into that huge task, he took a side path, "First, let me tell you about 'The Allegany 18': You pick up an 'Allegany 18' packet at the Red House Administration Building, hike 18 Park trails, fill out the forms in the packet, bring them back and you get your name in the registry and engraved on an 'Allegany 18' water bottle."

The Historical Society must have been tired. There was not a whole lot of energetic response but I will bet that when the word gets around, the "Allegany 18" will be the thing to do in the Park. The Adirondack 46ers have gotten people climbing out-of-the-way peaks all over the Eastern Adirondacks in pursuit of a badge that recognizes the achievement of climbing the 46 Adirondack peaks over 4,000 feet. "Allegany 18" should do it for the Park.'

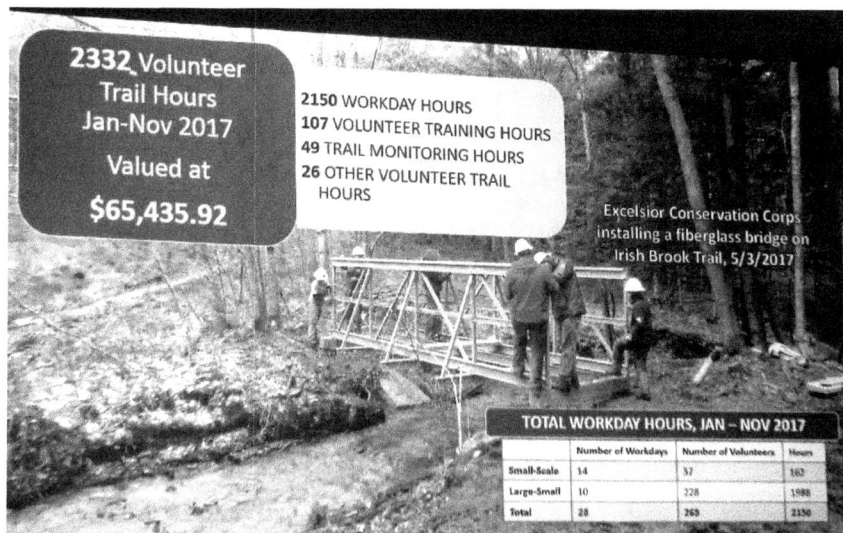

2332 Volunteer Trail Hours Jan-Nov 2017

Valued at

$65,435.92

2150 WORKDAY HOURS
107 VOLUNTEER TRAINING HOURS
49 TRAIL MONITORING HOURS
26 OTHER VOLUNTEER TRAIL HOURS

Excelsior Conservation Corps installing a fiberglass bridge on Irish Brook Trail, 5/3/2017

TOTAL WORKDAY HOURS, JAN – NOV 2017

	Number of Workdays	Number of Volunteers	Hours
Small-Scale	14	37	162
Large-Small	10	228	1988
Total	28	263	2150

Volunteers at Work

After that brief excursion, Patrick returned to the enormity of his job. "There are 250 miles of multiuse trails in the Park. Maintenance on the trails has been neglected for a long time. I am the only full-time employee assigned to trails. In the summer we hire three seasonal workers and last summer I had 10 volunteers. We had to give the volunteers First Aid training and teach them how to use chain saws but they were hard workers.

"We updated signs and repaired trails. Trail signs are in bad shape. Missing signs make it easy to get lost on hiking trails. I want signs at every juncture on every trail in the Park. People are getting lost on trails like on Eastwood Meadow. They wind up over in Bay State.

"The Park is loaded with trails. The Master Plan has loads of new trails that are still in the design stage. A week ago we had enough snow to run the Annual Cross Country Ski Race on the Art Roscoe Trail system. The snowmobilers are out there now waiting for snow. No snow now, but bikers and hikers will be in there soon. "

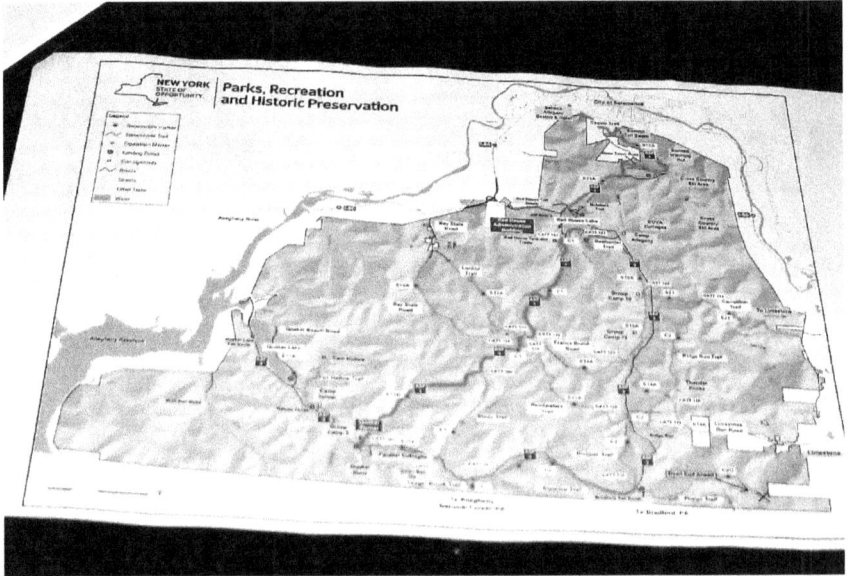

Allegany Trail Map

To indicate how many trails are available, Patrick indicated the pile of Cattaraugus County snowmobile trail maps he had stashed on one of the tables at the front of the room, along with Park hiking maps and equestrian trail brochures.

He continued, "We now have the Bear Paw Trail over toward the Stone Tower for snow shoe-ers. That way we avoid conflict with cross country skiers.

"Horse season begins May 15th and runs to November first." He pointed to Barney Weber in the audience. "Barney is in charge of the Equestrian Volunteers." We gave Barney a hand.

"The eight-mile, single-track Mountain Bike trail in the new Master Plan is on hold till we get the money for the heavy equipment it needs. In the meantime John Lundquist and his

Mountain Bike volunteers come and stay in the Summit Cabins three or four days every year and work on it."

Patrick's mention of a Mountain Bike trail would have brought on a vigorous discussion in Allegany National Forest or on Buffalo's Outer Harbor where Mountain Bikes have been bitterly opposed. The usual Mountain Bike Trail is narrow and one way. It is intended for a thrilling, high-speed ride twisting among trees, across planks and over jumps. It is dangerous to the rider and to hikers. The rush of traffic through a secluded wood is a major disturbance to the usual creatures that live there. Consider Googling "Mountain Bike videos" and judge for yourself whether the thrill ride is worth the sacrifice of healthy forest.

The Master Plan is a compromise between preservation of an invaluable resource and the recreational use of the resource. The blessing of the Master Plan is that although it allows exploitation like this Mountain Bike trail, it puts a limit on such exploitation. The Master Plan recognizes the unique quality of Allegany's forest and it protects that forest.

I raised my hand to get something going with, "Ski Patrol takes care of accidents on the cross-country ski trails. Mountain Biking is notorious for injuring people. What provisions are there for First Aid on the Mountain Bike Trail?"

Patrick passed my question to his boss, Tom Livak, who was in the audience. Tom described in detail the preparations Park Police have made for such emergencies as well as the new equipment they recently acquired.

Patrick asided, "Myself, I'm a hiker, number one. I love to hike. Before I took this job I went on a two-and-a-half-month back pack."

He came equipped with a slide show of work accomplished in 2017, titled, "Allegany Region Trails Maintenance and Development Summary," which he took us through.

There were pictures of all of these projects: a pedestrian footbridge on Mount Tuscarora, puncheon planking on Three Sisters Trail, directional signage in many places, resurfacing of the Irish Brook Road, fiberglass bridges on Black Snake Mountain and on Irish Brook, horse safety signs on Bay State Road and stairs on Black Snake Mountain.

One slide named six trails that Patrick and his crew had worked on: Red Jacket, Beehunter, Mount Tuscarora, Eastwood Meadows, Flagg, Three Sisters, Conservation and Osgood. I have hiked a few of them myself and that is a lot of mileage.

The slide listed the jobs accomplished on each. On the Mount Tuscarora Trail alone they cleared eighteen trees, installed two bridges, cut down a patch of stinging nettles, replaced the map at Coon Run, installed water control measures and built a stone turnpike. And that's a lot of work.

Patrick Dove with Rose and Lou Budnick

Patrick praised the "Allegany State Park Volunteer Trail Stewards program." One slide showed eight or nine of them in the woods working with long-handled tools, probably rakes. Another slide is filled with statistics describing their work. The most impressive statistic is that they cleared 42 downed trees. This slide also contains a photo of eight of the volunteers lined up in a formal pose and wearing uniform tee shirts.

Patrick fielded many questions from the audience:

"Yes, we have cleared vistas but we have to get permission from Albany to do it or to cut any trees.

"That old shanty is still up on Black Snake but it's about to fall down.

"We are building a Fisherman's Trail around Science Lake and we will mark 'The School in the Forest.'

"A water bar is a half-buried log to run water off the trail."

There were many more questions and very satisfactory answers.

Budnick's Delicious Apple Cake

Patrick had made it clear that one of his primary goals is good, careful trail marking. So trail markers make a good place to close. On the table in the front of the room he had placed a collection of plastic trail markers in red, yellow, maroon, blue and sky blue with horses, skiers, hikers and bikers depicted on them. Holding one of them up he said, "We put these markers every 30 meters along the trail. The trouble is that people take them home."

Someone in the audience said "They look like coasters. You should sell them in the Ad building."

Patrick said, "Yes, we thought of making them souvenirs.

"One time a kid was trying to get one off a tree on the trail, right in front of me. I asked him, 'What are you doing that for?'

"He said, 'I like to take one as a souvenir every time I hike a trail.'

"I had some in my pocket. I offered them to him. 'Here take one. It will save me putting up another one."

We applauded and came up front for more questions, another piece of Lou Budnick's apple cake…and maybe a souvenir to take home.

CONCLUSION

The land of the Allegany Oxbow has been used and abused. Its people have been removed from their lands. Those who took their place, were in turn removed.

Still, Allegany is beloved by all of them and by hundreds of thousands of the rest of us who come to the Park, only briefly, yet leave those shimmering lakes, towering forests and rolling mountains, with our spirits renewed.

www.ingramcontent.com/pod-product-compliance
Lightning Source LLC
LaVergne TN
LVHW051516080426
835509LV00017B/2081